ANTIFANATICISM:

A TALE OF THE SOUTH

AMS PRESS
NEW YORK

ANTIFANATICISM:

A TALE OF THE SOUTH.

BY

MISS MARTHA HAINES BUTT.

———◆———

PHILADELPHIA:
LIPPINCOTT, GRAMBO, AND CO.
1853.

Library of Congress Cataloging in Publication Data

Butt, Martha Haines, b. 1834.
    Antifanaticism: a tale of the South.

    1. Slavery in the United States--Fiction.
I. Title.
PZ3.B9804An6 [PS1235.B54]   813'.3   78-39571
ISBN 0-404-04575-8

.

Reprinted from an original copy in the collections of the
Wilbur L. Cross Library, University of Connecticut.

Reprinted from the edition of 1853, Philadelphia
First AMS edition published, 1973
Manufactured in the United States of America

AMS PRESS, INC.
New York, N. Y.   10003

TO

MRS. CAROLINE LEE HENTZ

Chis Work

IS INSCRIBED,

AS A TOKEN OF THE HIGHEST ESTEEM, BY HER FRIEND,

THE AUTHOR.

PREFACE.

Much has been said and written about the South by persons who never resided there, and who are ignorant of Southern feelings and Southern manners. Widely do these differ from those which such persons meet with in the frigid regions of the North. We greet each other, and the stranger, with warm sympathy, glowing hospitality, and a generous welcome, which makes the visitor at once feel at home under a Southern roof, and which assures him that the bosom warmed by such feelings cannot be the resting-place of cruelty and oppression.

Mrs. Stowe, and other fanatics, blinded by ignorance, and swayed by prejudice, may conjure up their "thousand and one" Uncle Tom stories, with which the imagination of novel-writers abounds, to deceive those who are as ignorant as themselves, and, perhaps, as reckless of truth; but no reasonable person, who has ever been at the South long enough to become acquainted with its usages, will give credit to the description which Mrs. Stowe, and those of her stripe, give of the treatment of slaves at the South. They are not mangled or cruelly tortured, as she represents in her work. It is not at all probable that a Southerner of refined and delicate feelings, and such are wealthy Southerners generally, would sell a much-valued slave, who had

1*

nursed him from his infancy, and also rescued the life of his child. No, no! So far from this, he would give him his freedom if he desired it, and something to begin the world with. But so attached does such a slave become to such an owner that he would not leave him on any consideration.

Many persons North are impressed with the idea that a southern plantation is a place of torture and cruelty, where slaves are driven like dogs, and never meet with a kind word or smile of approbation, however much it may be merited. On the contrary, nothing presents a more pleasing aspect than to see the respective cabins comfortably fitted up, with a little garden, or potato, or melon patch, attached. Everything around has the appearance of happiness. When the slaves have completed their daily toil, they retire to their quarters and enjoy a repast among themselves.

People of the North, who have never visited the South, should not give heed to stories which are but the figments of a worse than distempered imagination. Our slaves are infinitely better off than the white servants of the North. They have kind owners who care for them, and do all in their power to promote their happiness. When sick, they have prompt medical aid and kind nursing, as well as the counsel and prayers of humane and pious ministers. It is not the design of the author to exaggerate at all; what she states, she knows to be truth. She feels confident that the condition of slaves at the South is not what it has been represented by fanatical writers, as many a Northerner who has sojourned among us will bear witness.

The author was somewhat surprised to see what mistaken notions Mrs. Stowe has. She seems to think that our Southern people are under the impression that slaves have not immortal souls, susceptible of the sanctifying influence of grace here and glory hereafter. Could Mrs. Stowe but attend some of their religious meetings, and hear the songs of praise, the prayers, and even sermons of some of our slaves, she would think otherwise. Who taught those poor ignorant slaves the knowledge of God, and his Son, Jesus Christ? Not Northern men, but Southern masters, and Southern ministers; who, for their comfortable accommodation, as well as religious instruction, have erected suitable houses of worship, where the Sabbath, with all its high and holy delights, may be enjoyed.

The work before you is without any pretensions. It is the first attempt of a youthful author, who desires to deal justly and truly with the subject announced. She hopes her remarks will not create any unpleasant feelings among her Northern friends. She feels it her duty, as a warm-hearted Virginian, to defend the South, but, in so doing, she would not willingly offend the North.

MARTHA HAINES BUTT.

Norfolk, Va.

CONTENTS.

CHAPTER I.

CHAPTER VIII.

CHAPTER XVII.

CHAPTER XVIII.

CHAPTER XIX.

CHAPTER XX.

CHAPTER XXI.

CHAPTER XXII.

CHAPTER XXIII.

CHAPTER XXIV.

CHAPTER XXV.

ANTIFANATICISM;

A TALE OF THE SOUTH.

CHAPTER I.

SOUTHERN HOSPITALITY.

Mr. M—— was a wealthy planter at the South, and owned many slaves; he endeavored from their earliest years to impress them with the importance of being honest in all their dealings, and to act openly on all occasions. Often, he would visit their cabins, to see if all was going on right, offering his kind advice and aid. Whenever he was seen approaching the cabins, the inmates would all rush out, and each try to be the first one to welcome him to their little tenement.

His wife was a lady invested with high dignity of character, and commanded much respect from all around. The younger slaves were under her supervision, and each day it was her custom to instruct them in such things as would be of service in after life.

The mansion of Mr. M—— was, indeed, magnificent; everything that money could purchase was procured; yet, amid all these luxuries of life, he did not forget those who were dependent upon him. Possessed of high

2

integrity of character and benevolence of heart, he was ever ready to offer advice, and his purse was always open to the needy. As he viewed his extensive fields, he felt grateful that he had been so blessed by Providence, and showed his gratitude by a proper use of the same.

Medora (or Dora, as she was called) and Charles were the only children, and they were early taught to be kind to all, particularly the slaves. They were instructed never to show any feeling of superiority whatever toward the servants, but to treat them with civility. In consequence of manifesting such a disposition, they were loved by all. Often her nurse, old Aunt Phebe, would say, that "Miss Dora was de most politest child she eber seed, and if she lived she would make a mighty fine ooman." Charles was as great a favorite as his sister; he was never known to order the slaves about in a rude manner, but was always polite to them. Often he would go to old Uncle Dick, to get him to help him fly his kite, or tell him some of his marvellous tales, which he readily did, at the same time considering it a great honor. He labored under the impression that he was a powerful linguist; often when Charles would laugh at the droll pronunciation of his words, Uncle Dick would think he had said something very witty, and join heartily in the laugh.

One cold evening in midwinter, Mrs. M—— was seated before a large fire in the sitting-room. The lamps had just been lighted, making everything appear very cheerful. She was expecting her husband, who had been absent a week on a visit to his other plantations. She was anticipating his arrival home that evening. She had watched at the window until it had grown too dark to discern a single object.

She listened attentively to every sound, and soon the rattling of wheels was heard. She went to the door to meet her husband, and, much to her surprise, she saw a stranger with him. After the introduction, Mr. M—— related the circumstances which led to the meeting of this gentleman. The stranger he called Mr. I——. It appears that he had been travelling for quite a long time, and Mr. M——, noticing his fatigue, kindly invited him to remain at his home during the night. He knew there was no inn near, and the stranger needed rest, so he insisted that he should accompany him and remain at all events until the morning. Had it not been for the hospitality of Mr. M——, the stranger would have gone on his journey. They had by accident met each other, and, entering into conversation, it seems that a mutual friendship sprung up between them, and the stranger accepted the kind invitation of Mr. M——.

Mrs. M—— saw that everything was put in readiness for her guest. Soon, into a neatly-furnished room, in which a delightful fire of oak and lightwood was kindled, Mr. I—— was ushered, and told that that was his chamber for the night.

Oh! how cheering it was to the heart of the traveller; he felt deeply the kindness and hospitality of the South, and could not refrain from contrasting it with his northern home. "Who," thought he, "would be kind enough at the North to invite a stranger, one of whom he knew nothing, to share his home? How did this gentleman know but what I might have been a rogue? Ah, I see, he judges the world by himself, and he has such a noble heart, that he thinks all the world honest like himself."

Soon, his thoughts were interrupted by the ringing of the supper-bell. He was shown into the dining-room, where stood a table filled with every delicacy that heart could wish. Nice hot rolls, some of Aunt Chloe's best chicken, nicely broiled; smoking hot coffee, and everything else essential to a nice repast, which is so much relished by a hungry and fatigued traveller.

After they had finished, Mr. and Mrs. M—— entertained their visitor for some time. At length, Mr. M——, thinking that his guest must feel weary from travelling so long, proposed retiring. Mr. I—— entered his neatly-furnished chamber, and, in a very little while, he was slumbering sweetly, nor did he awaken until the sun poured brightly through the window the next morning.

Hearing a rap at the door he opened it, and found that Rufus had come for the purpose of kindling the fire. Rufus was one of the talkative kind, and whenever he found any one disposed to be loquacious, he generally took advantage of the opportunity.

" Massa, you Norrud gemman, ain't you?"

" Why do you think so, Rufus?"

"'Caze I hurd you and massa talking 'bout 'litionists last night, and den 'bout de slaves."

" Yes, Rufus, I am a Northerner, and am now on my way home. You seem to be well contented with your lot, Rufus."

" Yes sar; dis nigger neber leab his massa to go wid nobody; 'caze he know dat nobody ain't gwine to treat him good no how like massa does."

"Would you not like to be free, Rufus?"

"Well, I think not massa; 'caze den nobody would care for Rufus den—and when I be sick, no missus would be dar to tend poor Rufus. No! no! massa, me neber leab de souf in de world!"

"You are very happy, then?"

"Oh, yes! mighty happy; we all hab a dance ebery Saturday night, and I tell you what, if you was dar, I reckon how you would tink dat de debbil was tickling your heels, and, afore you knowed it, you would be dancing so—"

The conversation was interrupted by another rap at the door; Moses had been sent to tell Rufus to hurry and make the fire in the dining-room. They all knew Rufus well, and expected that he had stopped to have a chat with the gentleman; they were all pretty well aware of his propensity to talk.

After Rufus left the room, Mr. I—— pondered on the answer that he made him, and concluded, after all, that the slaves at the South were certainly far happier than they had been represented to be. He was highly delighted with the hospitality which had been shown him, and heartily wished that it was one of the characteristics of his own place; but, oh! thought he, there is a vast difference between the warm-hearted Southerners and the Northerners.

Soon breakfast was announced, and it consisted of the choicest dishes, for Aunt Phebe determined to try all her skill, and served up everything in the best style.

Mrs. M—— greeted him with a pleasing smile, and spared no pains to render herself particularly agreeable.

"I regret much, Mr. I——, that necessity compels you to leave us this morning. I was anxious that you should have a fair opportunity of visiting all around the plantation, and take a view of the cabins and their respective families. I know what a prejudice those North have of the Southerners because they are slave-holders, and they seem to think a plantation is nothing but a scene of cruelty and torture. I should be delighted if you could remain a while with us and judge for yourself, for I am well assured that the erroneous idea under which you labor would be eradicated at once.

Mr. I—— expressed a desire to remain longer, and stated that business called him home. He observed to Mrs. M—— her slaves seemed to be well contented with their lot, and related the conversation which had taken place between Rufus and himself during the morning. "I see, Mrs. M——, you are extremely indulgent to your slaves, and they all appear to love you; but I do not know whether to judge all the rest by yours or not."

Mrs. M—— replied, by saying that she was not an exception by any means, for there were many others who treated their slaves in the same manner as she did. She farther remarked, that she hoped Mr. I—— would endeavor to convince those around him what a mistaken idea they had with regard to slavery. She also gave him an invitation to make her house his home whenever occasion required that he should come that way, and promised to omit nothing on her part to render his visit agreeable.

Mr. I—— rendered his sincere thanks, and said, he would endeavor to arrange matters so as to come very soon, and bring his lady with him, and let her form an idea of southern hospitality.

They had been conversing for some time, and it was now getting quite late. Mr. M—— was at the stable giving directions about the horses, and having the carriage put in readiness which was to convey Mr. I—— to town. Having business there himself, he went with him, much to the gratification of Mr. I——, who had anticipated rather a monotonous ride. Soon all was in readiness, and, after taking leave of the children and Mrs. M——, they started.

During the ride, the conversation turned upon different subjects. Mr. I—— could scarcely talk of anything else but the hospitality of the South. It had really come so unexpected that he was wholly unprepared for anything of the sort. Mr. M—— remarked to him that hospitality was one of the greatest characteristics of the South, and was extremely happy to know that he had had a demonstration of the fact.

"But what do you think of the condition of the slaves South? I wish a candid opinion; do not be governed by anything but the dictates of your own heart; you are an abolitionist, of course."

Mr. I—— scarcely knew how to answer his friend, for really he was halting between two opinions. He had seen how perfectly happy the slaves of Mr. M—— appeared, and recollected the conversation between Rufus and himself.

After a few minutes' deliberation, he answered his friend by saying that he was almost inclined to believe the slaves happier than those who were free; for while under their owners they had some one to care for them, and to protect their rights.

He farther stated that he was an abolitionist, as might be expected, having been brought up at the North, and, as a natural consequence, imbibed their principles. "I should judge," said he, "from the bright countenances of your slaves, that they were perfectly contented. Last night I heard some one singing under my window, and another was playing on some musical instrument."

" I will venture to say that was Moses and Ben, for they often give me a serenade when I have been absent from home and return again."

It seems that Benjamin, or Ben, as he was called upon the plantation, thought himself quite a skilful performer on the banjo; and Moses, who prided himself upon his vocal powers, joined him.

Mr. I—— listened to them, and could not refrain from smiling at their grotesque appearance, standing under his window; Ben with his eyes rolled up, as if searching in the stars for his lady-love, sang " Dinah Crow," while Moses would join in the chorus, presenting a set of teeth having much the appearance of large grains of corn set in even rows.

Mr. I—— fell asleep with the words of " The belle of Louisiana" sounding in his ears. Moses, who had become so much carried away by the music, soon found himself dancing, in spite of the entreaties of Ben to " stop dat noise, for de gemman would wake up agin." At the same time, he was not aware what a noise his own voice made, his object was to be heard all himself.

The distance which Mr. M—— and his friend had to

ride was twelve miles; consequently, they had a fine opportunity of conversing upon different subjects.

The ride was fast coming to a close now, much to the regret of Mr. I——, who had passed such a pleasant time in the company of his friend. The stage which they were to meet was seen in the distance, and Mr. I—— could but express a regret at having to part with his companion, for he well knew how monotonous several hours' ride in the stage would be. "But," thought he, "I shall fall in with some one, and shall be agreeably disappointed in my stage ride after all.

His thoughts were soon interrupted by the rattling of wheels, and now Rufus jumps down to open the carriage door.

After a pressing invitation to Mr. M—— to make him a visit, and telling him that although where he lived they did not possess the same hospitality as he had found at the South, yet he would imitate the manners of the Southerners, and, when he came, he would be as much pleased with his visit North as he was South.

"All aboard!" echoed in the ears of Mr. I——, and in a few minutes the stage disappeared.

In the stage there happened to be some very strong abolitionists, in company with some Southerners. The slave question (which is a Northerner's hobby) came up, of course.

"I think," said one, "that something ought to be done to put a stop to this slave business; I think it a disgrace to the whole community. Poor creatures, they are doomed to drudge and toil, and are cruelly beaten after all."

"Yes," replied a merchant (who then had poor boys

employed in his establishment at only four shillings a week), "I think it shameful; and, if I had my way, I would put a stop to it. They have as much right to be free as ourselves, and they should enjoy their freedom."

One of the Southerners, who had been listening until he felt the very blood curdle in his veins, now could stand it no longer. "I would like to know what you call humanity, Mr. Northerner. I wonder if you Northerners do not employ people to work for you from morning till night, and then what remuneration do you give them? Some are put off with only one dollar a week, and with that they have to clothe themselves. I should think that a small sum, indeed, for the poor creatures; they can scarcely obtain enough to satisfy their demands. Sir, do not talk to me about your Northern humanity, when I have seen so much misery and suffering among the white slaves. There are many of them who would gladly live in the cabins of our slaves, and feel themselves blessed with what my slaves possess. The abolitionists are very willing to get the slaves from their masters; but, if they come to want, they are the first ones to turn them from their doors."

The Northerner's lips were closed completely; he must have felt the strength and truth of the Southerner's remarks, and his conscience smote him.

Mr. I——, who had been listening very attentively to the conversation, spoke: "I have just returned from a place where I never saw, in all my life, so much hospitality. It was at a wealthy planter's, surrounded by a quantity of slaves, and they all appeared to be perfectly happy."

"But they might have assumed that air, through fear of their master."

"No, no, sir; I had a conversation with one in my room, with the door shut; no one was in hearing; and he actually told me that he did not desire his freedom, and he was as happy as he could be."

Another Northerner, who thought himself very witty, replied: "You know the reason that Jack did not eat his supper?"

"Now, listen to me a moment, sir," said Mr. I——; "I am from the North myself, and he knew that I could make a way easy enough for him to get away, if he were disposed to go. But he told me that he would never leave his master. That just convinces me at once that slavery at the South is not what it has been represented to be. Just look around at the neat little cabins, and hear them all singing at night, around a cheerful wood-fire. They have the night to themselves; you know that our white slaves have to work at night as well as in the day."

"Well, really, I believe the Southerners have prose-lyted you; but you need not believe all that they tell you."

"No, you are mistaken; they have only proved to me, by their hospitality, and kind treatment to their slaves, that I was laboring under a wrong impression altogether."

The parties commenced to get quite enthusiastic upon the subject on which they were conversing, and the time passed off so rapidly, that they were not aware of its flight until they saw that night was now drawing its sombre mantle around them. Soon they discovered houses; hence they knew that their stage journey was drawing to an end. In a short time the inn met their eye, and it was welcome, indeed. It was quite cold, and their appetites became keen, for it had been some time since they had eaten anything. Now, regaling themselves with hot coffee, and edibles, we leave them to enjoy their repast, while we describe Aunt Phebe's cabin.

CHAPTER II.

AUNT PHEBE'S CABIN.

Mr. M—— had an old and favorite servant, whose name was Phebe. She had been Dora's nurse, but, since she had grown large enough to do without any looking after, Aunt Phebe turned cook. It would do any one good just to take a peep at her cabin, so neatly furnished, and see all the tin and kitchen utensils, in first-rate order, shining on the shelves. Now, Aunt Phebe was one of that kind who can do a little of everything; she was a beautiful washer and ironer, an excellent cook and house-servant. All on the plantation had a great respect for Aunt Phebe, and looked upon her as something wonderful.

We will just take a peep into her cabin, while she is preparing supper, and see how nicely all things go on. Aunt Phebe had a very high opinion of herself, and, if you were just to listen at the door for a few minutes, you would often hear her praising herself. Look at her, with her nice head-handkerchief of blue and yellow, starched as stiff as it could well be, and tied upon her head. Watch her, as she smiles when she opens the oven and peeps in at the rolls. "Dese rolls, Phebe'd like to see de nigger dat could beat 'em; and dat ar' flannel-cake, it am de tiptop. Dis Phebe she knows how to make 'em. Massa Charlie always say dat Aunt

3

Phebe makes biscuit light 'nuff to send 'em, wid a puff ob de bref, in de air." Aunt Phebe, hearing a titter in the corner, turns round. "You Mose, dat you? I'll crack yer head if I comes dar, you audacious villain. I'll let you see I ain't gwine to stand dat ar' 'purtinence. You Cary, git me dat vip, and I'll gib it to you, sar, right cross yer mouf."

Aunt Phebe's menaces always proved effectual, for a little while, at least; it would serve to silence the urchins a few minutes. But not very long did it last, for Cary gives Moses a slap, and then Aunt Phebe comes down upon them with a vengeance.

"Yer Mose, I be de def of yer yit; wait till I gits dis supper in de house, and den yer see if I don't pay yer off!"

Aunt Phebe was fussing away around the fire getting the supper in readiness, when old Uncle Dick comes in—

"I say, ole ooman, what's de matter now? ain't de rolls riz? Wait till I gets a peep at 'em!"

With this, Uncle Dick takes the lid off and looks in; Aunt Phebe breaks out upon him: "I tells yer what, ole man, yer see I don't tank yer for lettin' all de steam out dem dar rolls by taking de lid off, 'caze I want mindin' 'bout dem, no how; I was tinking 'bout dese young 'uns I'se gwine to crack 'em good!"

"Now don't begin to scold, ole ooman, I only wanted to see how dey looked!"

Aunt Phebe was quite subdued by Uncle Dick's reply, and said, "that she thought dat flannel-cake would beat eberyting she eber seed in all her life."

"Here it comes! here it comes!" cries Moses and Cary.

"Lord bless dem chil'en, dey makes more noise dan a little; to be sure and sartin, de debbil must be comin'. Let me see," said Uncle Dick, "what is comin'? Why, its massa; whar' he bin?"

"Hurry up, ole ooman, its time de supper was gwine in; I knows massa hungry, 'caze dis here cold air sorter gibs one a relish!"

"Whar's massa bin?" again asked Uncle Dick.

"Why, he went wid dat 'litionist yesterday to carry him to town. I b'lieve he jist did it to keep him company, an' I bound yer don't ketch dis here nigger hab-ing nuffin' to do wid 'em. I b'lieves in my soul dat he was tryin' to 'suade Rufus off. But Rufus time nuff for him den."

Uncle Dick had not been home for a day or two, and knew nothing of Mr. I——'s visit. Mr. M—— had told Uncle Dick that, whenever he had no employment for him he might do something for himself, so he had been at the neighboring plantation working in order to earn a little money. He was quite advanced in years now, so Mr. M—— did not exact much from him; he had served him faithfully, he would have given him his freedom, but Uncle Dick had told him that he would rather remain with him because he would be better taken care off.

Aunt Phebe had now sent the supper in, and is busy in preparation of her own. Uncle Dick, whose appetite the ride had somewhat sharpened, now began to make inquiries respecting his supper.

"I say, ole ooman, what yer got to night? I fotch

home some chickens which I bought at de plantation wid de money dey paid me for sawing de wood."

"Whar's dey?" asked Aunt Phebe, who was not a little delighted at the idea of having nice broiled chicken for supper.

"Well, ole man, if yer has no 'jections, I'll jist wring de neck ob dis here 'un, and I'll set de young 'uns to fotch some water to scald dem in to take off de ferrus."

"Agreed!" said Uncle Dick, who felt as if he would like to make a supper off the chicken, but was a little afraid to broach the subject to Aunt Phebe, as he had not found her in the best humor in the world.

Aunt Phebe busied herself awhile preparing the chicken, and then set her table, spreading a nice white cloth upon which were placed shining knives and forks. In a short time supper was in readiness; Aunt Phebe, Uncle Dick, and the children seated themselves.

Moses and Cary were evidently much delighted at the sight of the chicken, and Aunt Phebe had to set them to rights by giving them an occasional crack with the handle of her fork.

Cary was so eager to make his supper, that he upset a cup of coffee over the white tablecloth, much to the displeasure of Aunt Phebe, who had a great mind, she said, to send them off to bed wid no supper at all.

Uncle Dick never left Aunt Phebe a day or two without bringing her something when he returned; it was always her custom to ask ole man what he had fotched for her. Uncle Dick brings out a huge bundle, and, on opening it, it was found to contain some lightwood, a pipe, and some tobacco.

Aunt Phebe's eyes brightened at the sight of the new

pipe and tobacco; the former she placed in her mouth, and went before the glass to see how it looked.

"You's mighty wain, ole ooman," said Uncle Dick; "I seed you more dan once looking in dat ar' glass, but I tell yer what, when I was courtin' yer I did tink yer was de purtiest cretur I eber did see. But didn't I war de standin' collar den, and de studs in my shirt bosom?" Uncle Dick was evidently waiting to hear himself complimented, but Aunt Phebe was too much taken up with the thoughts how beautiful she used to be, to make any answer.

"Uncle Dick! Uncle Dick!" cries Charlie, "I want to see you!"

"Lor' bless my soul, if dat ain't massa Charlie callin' me; I ain't seed de dear child for dese two days. Open de door, Mose!"

Charlie enters, puffing and blowing as if he had been running a mile.

"Where have you been all this time, Uncle Dick? You don't know how much I missed you yesterday; I wanted you to help me to fly my kite, for I did not have any one to assist me, so I had to put it back in its place."

"Whar' was Rufus?"

"He went with papa to town."

"Yes, yes, so he did!"

"The others, you know, were so busy that they could not help me. Well, where have you been all this time, Uncle Dick?"

"I went ober to dat ar' plantation on the tother side to saw wood; massa told me how when I habs nuffin' much to do for him I kin work a little for myself. Yer

3*

know, Massa Charles, dat Uncle Dick is gettin' old now, and it won't be berry long afore he is gwine to start on his long journey. I feels dese feeble limbs growing weaker ebery day; by and by yer see ole Uncle Dick no more ; you stand by his grave and say, dar poor ole Uncle Dick lays ; he help me once to fly my kite, but he help me no longer!"

Charlie felt sad whenever he heard him talk so, and never left him in a solemn mood, but would always make him tell some little story. Uncle Dick had the art of embellishing to a great extent, and he knew very well what kind of a story to tell in order to please him.·

"Uncle Dick, I am afraid you are tired, and I won't trouble you any longer; you must go to bed now."

" Well, massa, I do feel tired, for my poor old limbs won't stand much; but, if you has a mind to stay, I will be glad on it. Don't hurry yourself on my account."

"I will go now, Uncle Dick ; and some night, when you are not tired, I will come again. Good-night, Uncle Dick; good-night, Aunt Phebe."

" Good-night, massa."

"Ain't dat ar' child one angel? Jist hear how he talks. Ain't he got a kind heart? Massa talks 'bout sendin' him 'way. I hopes he ain't gwine to send him 'fore I die, no how."

" Dat child is a 'ception, sure," said Aunt Phebe; "he an' Miss Dora both is mighty good chil'en, and massa and missus both will be proud on 'em some day."

Uncle Dick had been thinking about the " 'litionist," as he called him, ever since he heard Aunt Phebe say he had been there. His feelings always revolted at the idea of them. Hearing Rufus whistling, he called him in, to hear the particulars.

"I say, Rufus, I hurd dat massa had a 'litionist to see him."

"Egad! and he did; but didn't dis nigger talk to him? I b'lieves in my heart he wanted to try to 'suade me off; but I be time nuff for him den."

"I tink myself, dat when he gits 'head ob you dat he ain't got but one more to come over, and dat is de debble. What did you say to him?"

"Why, I jist told him I wouldn't leab massa nohow; 'caze he was good to me, an' dat de white folks Norf treated de white sarvants bad 'nuff, and dat if dey got one wid a black skin dey would be de def on him."

"You jist told him right, Rufus."

Aunt Phebe had been listening for some time, but had not said a word. At last she broke her silence:—

"I hurd him de tother mornin', when I went to carry de cakes in at breakfast, ax if we sarvants was happy. Massa tole him yes; and I do wish it hadn't been onpolite for me to jine in, I bound I would have told him fast 'nuff what I thought ob de 'litionists. I had to come away, for I really was afear'd dat I would speak anyhow. So I gibed Rufus de cakes at de door, and he carried them in."

"For my part, ole ooman, I tinks we be better off dan dem free niggers what dey habs Norf; 'caze, arter dey wars out one suit ob clothes dey don't know whar' de tother is comin' from. We's got a kind massa, who gibs us dem, when we needs 'em. Don't talk to me 'bout dem 'litionists, dey don't know nuffin 'bout dese slaves. I guess dey don't see dis nigger gwine away wid none ob dem."

Uncle Dick, who was now getting quite sleepy, did not know exactly how to get around to give Rufus the hint to go. After a little while he thought of a way.

"You see, Rufus, I'se an ole man now, and can't stand much, like you young folks. I don't want to be onpolite, but den I must ax you to go, and come again when I feels rested. Young massa was here a while ago, and he told me dat he knowed I was tired, and dat I must go to bed now."

Rufus, who was very polite on all occasions, now told Uncle Dick that it needed no 'pologies whatever, and dat he ought to hab giben de hint afore. After wishing them a good-night, he left them to enjoy a repose from the labors of the day.

Rufus was always a great favorite of Aunt Phebe's, and she having some of his clothes to put in order, she sat up for some time to fix them.

As we have said, Aunt Phebe was much inclined to talk to herself; while she was sitting there, she would say something about "dat 'litionist." Soon a kind of drowsiness came over her, and her head went from one side to the other, and then against the wall, with quite a bump; at which Aunt Phebe jumped up, screaming out, and said that the "'litionist was gwine to kill her."

Uncle Dick, who was aroused by her noise, became quite provoked, and said that he wished "ole ooman would let de 'litionists alone, and den she wouldn't be bustin' her head open agin de wall 'bout 'em, and not be wakin' him up arter he had got to sleep." But, as it was not a very difficult matter for him to get asleep, he was soon off again.

And now, Aunt Phebe, we leave you for the night, and hope that the morning will find you with your head safe upon your shoulders, in spite of the unmerciful bump it received against the wall.

CHAPTER III.

LITTLE HANNAH.

NEXT in importance on the plantation stood Aunt
Nelly. She had been living for many years with Mrs.
M——, so a pretty strong attachment was formed be-
tween her and her mistress.

Old Aunt Nelly had been much afflicted by losing her
children, and now only one remained. She was called
Hannah, being a favorite name of Aunt Nelly's. It
was a puny, delicate little creature, and but for the
constant care of Mrs. M——, she would have fallen a
prey to disease. She was a sort of playmate, there
being no other female child upon the plantation.

Little Hannah was what might be called really pretty;
her features very small and regular, her eyes were bright
and as black as ebony. Her meekness and amiability
endeared her to her mistress, who watched her with all
care. Gradually her health improved, until at last Mrs.
M—— thought her perfectly restored. Dora was as
much delighted with the change as her mother, and
would sometimes say, in her childlike manner: " Hannah shall be my dressing-maid, when she gets large
enough."

But troubles come upon us when least expected.
Little Hannah, whom they all thought in a fair way for

recovery, was taken suddenly ill, and, after lingering for but a few days, died. It was really distressing to hear poor Aunt Nelly talk. She had lost many children, and now this was her last one. Oh! how reluctantly did she give it up, and what grief filled her breast, as she watched life fast declining. Dora was very attentive at her bedside, and one night she begged her mother so imploringly to allow her to sit up, that she consented.

Dora was sitting by her the evening that she died; she had been told by her mother that little Hannah would not remain long with her. The child sat there very thoughtfully, and, after a while, she said, "Hannah, they tell me that you are going to die. Oh! I wish you could live until I am a grown lady. I would treat you just as mamma does!"

"Don't grieve for Hannah, Miss Dora, I am going home to heaven. I dreamed last night that I saw a little angel beckoning to me. I love you, Miss Dora, but must leave you soon. I hope to meet you in heaven." Suddenly, she ceased speaking. Dora took up her hand, which had wasted away so rapidly in a few days; it was icy cold; oh, how her heart bled at the sight. She turned from the bed on which little Hannah was lying and wept aloud. But the spirit of the little one had soared to heaven; and now, perchance, it looked down upon those who were mourning her loss.

Aunt Nelly was inconsolable. Her mistress sympathized deeply with her, but her grief was too great to be healed, and time was the only thing which could moderate it in the least.

The next day Dora went to look at the corpse; she plucked a simple white rose from the conservatory and placed it upon her bosom. It seemed as though it was the last thing which she could do, and it gave her heart delight.

Hannah's death spread quite a gloom over all on the plantation; the dance which they were to have on the birthnight of Rufus, which was but a week off, was deferred. Dora, too, who intended giving a party, although the invitations were out, gave up the idea. The neat white dress which Mrs. M—— made for little Hannah to wear on the occasion (for Dora intended that she should wait upon her company), served for a shroud.

After the death of little Hannah, Dora seemed very lonely indeed. She would take her dolls from the play-house and insist upon her mother's making black dresses for them. Mrs. M——, seeing her child's grief, would do anything to please her, or divert her mind from the loss with which she had met.

Time, which assuages grief, served to modify that of Dora; yet, at the same time, she never forgot little Hannah. Often she would go to the grave with Aunt Nelly on Sabbath evenings. Uncle Dick, in his rambles, found a beautiful double cape jasmine, which comes to such a perfection at the South, and planted it upon the grave. The first flower which it bore was hailed with delight, and Dora would have considered it a sacrilege to have plucked it, although she so much desired to show it to her mother. Mrs. M——, who ever sought to gratify every wish of her daughter, had a neat headstone placed at the grave, with a simple inscription carved upon it. Uncle Dick put a little railing around it, and planted some grass-seed, which came up in the spring, presenting a very beautiful appearance.

It is true that little Hannah was a slave, yet she was far happier than many who are free. What was the difference? It is true that she did not have what is called freedom, in the general acceptation of the term, yet she enjoyed all those pleasures which are known to those who are born free.

This incident of the death of little Hannah is not an exception ; no, no, there are thousands of slaves at the South cared for as much, and their death lamented in the same manner. Dora's affection for the little slave is not one in a thousand; no, but nine hundred out of a thousand.

Mrs. M—— sympathized with Aunt Nelly truly, for she well knew that slaves are capable of receiving as much pleasure and pain as ourselves. Hence, whenever, she found any of her slaves in trouble or distress, she would offer her friendly aid willingly.

Mrs. M——, seeing how much grieved Aunt Nelly was about the loss with which she had met, endeavored to think of some way to divert her mind. Mrs. M—— could devise no other plan than going to L—— for a few days; she thought that, perhaps, change of scene and air would be of service to her. So she told her to pack all things in readiness, and they would start in a day or two.

Although Aunt Nelly did not anticipate much pleasure from the trip, yet she thought it might serve to divert her mind a little.

It happened that, on her way, she met with a woman

4

about her own age, who had had a young child stolen
from her by the abolitionists. The poor mother was
dreadfully distressed, and said that she would rather
she were dead than for her to be in their power.

Aunt Nelly felt that her little Hannah was infinitely
better off, and compared the case of the woman with
that of her own. She knew that little Hannah was in
heaven now, and free from all sin.

By the time Mrs. M——'s visit was out, Aunt Nelly's
grief had subsided in a measure, for she had done all
in her power to cheer her up.

Since the death of Hannah, Dora had become still
dearer to Aunt Nelly, who had always loved her fondly
from infancy. She never looked at her now, but what
she thought of her own child, and how much she used
to love Dora.

One evening, Mr. and Mrs. M—— were in the sitting-
room conversing upon different subjects. "I have been
thinking," said Mr. M——, "some time that I would
give Nelly her freedom. Since the death of her child,
she seems so forlorn that it makes me heartily sorry to
look at her. She has been a faithful servant many years,
and now I will offer her her freedom."

Mrs. M—— readily consented, and said, "Perhaps
it might serve to restore her former spirits. I will
speak to her about it to-morrow, and hear what she has
to say."

After breakfast, the following day, Mr. M—— sent
for Aunt Nelly. She soon made her appearance.

"I intend, Nelly, to give you your freedom," said
Mr. M——, "and then you can do just as you wish."

At this, Aunt Nelly was completely astonished, and

began to think she had offended her master, and he wished to get clear of her.

"Why, lor' bless me, massa, what has poor ole Nelly done to yer, sar?"

Mr. M—— could scarcely refrain from laughing; he replied, "Nothing, my good woman; I wanted to give you your freedom because you have been so faithful, and behaved yourself so properly. Do you desire your freedom, Nelly?"

"Well, massa, I don't want to leab yer, and if yer gib me my freedom, why den I 'spose I'll hab to leab yer."

"Oh, no! Nelly, not by any means. If I were to give you your freedom, and I should happen to die, then you could go where you wished."

"Massa, I tell yer what yer can do; yer jist keep all de free papers; and if yer die, den yer can gib em to me if yer sees fit. Nelly don't want 'em now, 'caze she is free enough already."

"I declare," said Mr. M——, after Aunt Nelly left the room; "she is a faithful old creature. I know that she is as happy as she can be, yet I thought I would give her her freedom. One good thing, she knows very well that she can obtain it at any time."

Aunt Nelly went to Aunt Phebe's cabin, and the first question of course was: "Well, Nelly, what did massa want wid yer?"

"He axed me if I wanted my freedom, and if I did he would gib it to me, but I told him dat I was free 'nuff."

"I tink so, too," said Uncle Dick, "and I neber intend to leab massa while I lib."

"What did you tell him?" asked Rufus.

"I jist said dat I wa'n't gwine to leab him, but if he had de free papers he might keep 'em, and den if anyting happened, and he seed proper, why den he mought gib 'em to me."

"Dat's de bery question dat ar' 'litionist axed him, if we didn't want to be free?"

"I jist told him dat I was happy 'nuff, and so was all de rest of us."

Soon a signal from the overseer reminded them that they were to go to their respective labors.

They all obeyed immediately, going along singing merrily to their work. Even a lord might have wished to be thus happy.

What added much to their merriment was its being Saturday. It was the custom of Mr. M—— to allow them the privilege of retiring two hours sooner from their labor on that day, so that they could have an opportunity of having some part of the day to themselves.

Aunt Phebe, with a large tub of water and her scrubbing-brush, sleeves rolled up, gets down on the floor and scrubs away for life, as if determined that it shall be as bright as her own face.

Moses and Cary are sent in quest of white sand to sprinkle upon the floor. The day previous, Aunt Phebe always put the cooking utensils in fine order, so as to have more time on Saturday. How the tins all shone, and how white the wooden trays look! She was one of the kind who had a place for everything; and everything was kept in its place.

After regaling herself with her pipe, and looking over the clothes of the children and Uncle Dick, to see that they are in readiness for the coming day, she goes to work to prepare her mistress's supper, with a cheerful heart singing the while.

Nor does Uncle Dick leave anything undone; he takes a chicken or two from the coop and wrings the neck for Aunt Phebe, so that after she has got through with supper she can prepare it for cooking.

Really, a Saturday night on the plantation of Mr. M—— is a scene of pleasure; it would do any one good just to take a peep into each cabin, and see them all seated by a cheerful fire—some with pipes in their mouths, while others are feasting.

Among the younger slaves there was quite a good deal of sport there, for they usually had a dance, which was done up in "de fust style," as Rufus used to say, who was generally the head one there.

They all thought Rufus could outdance anything, for he fairly made the ground shake.

"Missus, but den I lubs dat ar' Ben; an' don't he play on de banjo do? I tinks dat ar' nigger beats all I eber seed."

With this Lizzie commenced dancing, imagining that she heard Ben playing on the banjo.

"You are willing to go, then, Lizzie?" said her mistress.

"Yes, marm!"

"I will tell you what I will do; I did think, at first, that I would sell you to him; but now I think differently. I will give you your freedom."

"Den I kin go to Ben!"

"Yes, certainly you can!"

"Will Mr. M—— give Ben his'n?"

"His what?"

"Why, his liberty, marm!"

"Yes, that is just what he is going to do."

"Well, what did she say about it?" said Mr. B——
to his wife, after the interview with Lizzie.

"Oh, she is willing to go; it is true that she regrets
leaving us, but then you know how it is; her affections
are centred upon Ben, and it is perfectly natural that
she should wish to go."

"I thought that I would not sell her; I will give her
her freedom. What do you say to it?"

"That is just what I said to her this morning; she
is delighted at the idea."

"Well, I will just go over and inform Mr. M——.
I told him that I would let him know this afternoon
about it."

Mr. B—— made all possible haste to inform Mr.
M—— of his intentions regarding the servant.

"I spoke to her," said he, "this morning; and I
think, from what he told me, that Ben generally gave
them music from his banjo." Sometimes they would
all get into such glee when dancing! Ben would stop
the banjo for a few minutes, but they all went on dancing just the same, for they thought he was playing.
Ben would laugh heartily to himself and say, "What
fools dem niggers is; dey ain't got 'nuff sense to know
when de music stops." He would take good care, though,
to resume the music in a little while, lest he should spoil
the joke, for he saw the eyes of Rufus rolling that way
more than once. They would dance around a large fire
kindled out doors; the cool air would make them move

more quickly, and the bright flames flickered, presenting a very cheerful aspect.

Mrs. M—— could see them dancing from her window, when it was moonlight, and she would often sit there and watch them, being very much amused as she saw Ben playing with all his might upon the banjo.

Rufus, who was always very gallant, and tried to be very polite on all occasions, was paying his devoirs to Laura. She had endeavored to render herself particularly agreeable that night, and had ornamented herself with all her trinkets. A deep blue rose was placed in her coal-black hair, which Rufus thought was natural.

"Lah, Rufus! I tought you had better sense dan dat; whar' did you eber see a blue rose natural?"

The dance ceasing for awhile, he led Laura to the cabin and took his seat by her. He had been rolling his great eyes around at her the whole evening, and Laura began to think herself quite beautiful. Rufus, wishing to make as great a display as possible, drew from his pocket a blazing red pocket-handkerchief bordered with yellow, and passed it across his mouth.

The sight of it took Laura's eyes. She "railly tought (as she told Rufus) dat he was de most tastical gemman she eber did see."

Rufus's design was accomplished, for he had taken it from his pocket for no other purpose than to have it admired.

Hearing the banjo strike again, they all proceeded to arrange themselves around the fire which had been replenished. Rufus was "mighty 'fraid (so he said) dat Miss Laura's frock would cotch a fire, for she was turning round dar at a great rate." Every limb was in motion; even Ben, who was playing upon the banjo, found himself dancing.

During all this time, Aunt Phebe and Uncle Dick were sitting around the fire in their own cabin; hearing such a dancing, and thinking that they must all be in a great glee, Aunt Phebe ventured out to see them, but the cool air soon caused her to return again and take her accustomed seat by the fire.

"I tell yer what, ole ooman, does yer want to git de rumatiz? I tink her does, or yer wouldn't be running arter dem young folks; yer know yer ain't like dem. But I seed de time when yer could beat 'em all hollow, I tell yer; an' dis old Dick, he could outshine dat Rufus any time when he got on de standin' collar and pumps, but couldn't he, den!"

"Don't talk of dem days," said Aunt Phebe; "I wish dese here niggers could only hab seen us when we was gwine to church; didn't I look purty wid my white wail on? I tell 'em what, I made de nigger star'.

"I do wonder if dey ain't gwine to stop dat dancin' to-night? I 'spects not, if Rufus habs anyting to do wid it, for yer jist ought to hab seen de lovation he was carryin' on wid Laura! Lor's a massy, but didn't she larf when Rufus kissed her hand? She say, 'Rufus, I'll slap yer right cross yer mouf de next time yer do dat,' and den she knowed dat she was glad 'nuff ob it. If dat ar' Rufus ain't de most foolishest nigger I eber did see; dis night air is gwine to git all de stiffenin' out his shirt-collar, and I know I ain't gwine to be starchin' all de week to hab it all tuck out on Saturday night. Wonder if dat ar' check collar won't do as well; I see de bottom ob it all now, he tought Laura would tink him mighty rich to be warring dem white standin' collars, but I knows if de starch does git out, and it hangs like dog yars, I ain't gwine to let him hab de tother."

The slaves having kept up the dance for some time, now felt a little fatigued, so they returned from the dancing-ring for the night.

In spite of everything, Miss Laura thinks she must faint, she is so overcome with dancing. Rufus, now as gallant as ever, and showing much anxiety, runs and gets his large straw hat that he wears in the summer, which serves in the place of an umbrella, and commences to fan her. She now throws her head back, displaying every tooth she has in it, while Rufus is dreadfully frightened lest she should faint.

Ben, with mouth open, looks upon the scene with astonishment, and wonders "what is de matter wid dat ar' foolish nigger, and dat he wan't gwine to play de banjo no more, if all dat 'fectation was to come arter."

"I say, Rufus, what's de matter wid dat ar' gal?"

"Why, don't yer see, she is gwine to faint!".

"Well, what on earth did yer git dat ar' great hat of your'n out for. I 'spose yer will fotch de water in dat to throw on her if she faints?"

"No, you foolish nigger, don't yer see I got it to fan her wid!"

After Rufus had fanned Laura as much as she desired, she came to, much to the delight of Rufus, who had begun to think that she never would recover, and said "dat he was tired fanning on her."

Laura, hearing this, thought that she would show some of her spirit, and said : "If yer don't want to fan me, yer can let it alone !"

Rufus, now more amazed than ever, replied : "Why, bless my heart, I thought yer had fainted, and when folks faints dey can't hear what is gwine on !"

"You are a cuteful nigger, Rufus !"

" I beg yer pardon a thousand times, Miss Laura ; dis here nigger (pointing to Ben) wexed me, and it made me mad."

Laura was a little subdued by the loving looks of Rufus, and told him that he was very 'scusable, and she would think nothing more of it.

As it was getting quite late, they all separated for the night. Rufus kissed the hand of Laura and told her "dat he was gwine to dream of her dat night, and she must dream of him."

Aunt Phebe declared that she was heartily glad "dat dem niggers had done der tarnation fuss, 'caze dey would let her hab no rest, and she 'spected dat dey would dance demselves to def anyhow."

But very soon after they all separated, and a profound quietude prevailed upon the plantation. Dancing so long had caused them to become quite drowsy, and it was not long before they were sleeping quite soundly. As for Rufus, we will say that it was some time before his thoughts would let him sleep ; he could think of nothing else but how pretty Laura looked with the blue rose in her hair, and of how angry she got with him for saying he was tired of fanning her. With the image of Laura before his eyes, he fell asleep and dreamed all night about the beautiful blue rose she had worn in her hair that night, and he awakened himself the next morning by fanning himself furiously with his great straw-hat, dreaming at the same time that Laura had fainted again, and he was employed in the very agreeable task of fanning her.

But very soon a loud rap at the door brought him to himself; it was Aunt Phebe, who asked him if he was gwine to sleep all de day 'caze it was Sunday.

Now, with the delightful thought of seeing Laura that day, he was out of his cabin in a very few moments. He was a little put, however, at the looks of his shirt-collar, for sure enough, as Aunt Phebe had said, it hung like dog's ears, but he knew what he would get if he went to her with any of his complaints, so he thought it better to wait for some auspicious moment and he would get around her, and after all get another stiff standing-collar; sure enough, too, he accomplished his design, and now, dressed up to kill, he goes to see how Miss Laura is to-day.

She, who had anticipated his company of course, put on her best looks, and Rufus declared that he never saw her look so pretty in all his life. "Why, you looks like a pink, to-day, Miss Laura; you must hab knowed I was comin' for sure. But whar's de blue rose?"

"Why, Rufus, you didn't tink I was gwine to war' it to day, did you?"

To please Rufus, she, in spite of herself, had to put it on her bonnet when she went to take the promised walk with her lovely Rufus.

CHAPTER IV.

MADORA.

TIME passed on very rapidly, and Madora was getting to be quite a large girl. Mrs. M—— thought it advisable to send her away to school. She was well aware of the importance of an education, and had determined to spare no pains nor expense to have her mind thoroughly cultivated. She knew it was best that she should send Madora away from her, for awhile at least. It would give her an opportunity of seeing more of the world, and also learn her to appreciate her home. Surrounded as she was by every luxury, and kind parents who gratified her every want, she knew nothing of the sorrows of the world, and, if they should happen to come upon her, she was ill-fitted indeed to receive them. Her mother thought much upon these things, so, with the consent of her husband, determined to send her away in the spring. Anything like novelty always delights children; so when Mrs. M—— mentioned to Madora that she was going away to school, she was delighted, and ran immediately to tell Aunt Phebe.

"Why, bless my soul, an' massa's gwine to send you away! Who will poor Phebe hab to lub her now?"

"But, Aunt Phebe, I will love you then as much as I do now, and I won't be gone long. When I come back I will be a larger girl, and mamma says I learn in great big books, and when I come home she will be so proud of me."

"Ah, honey! I'se afraid dat larnin' in dem ar' big books, as you call 'em, will make you forget all 'bout Aunt Phebe; and when yer comes back yer will be too big for me to nuss."

"But, Aunt Phebe, you will be quite old, then, and I can nurse and take good care of you."

"De Lord bless dat chil', I does lub her, and I don't want missus to be sendin' her away among dem Norrud folks no how, I don't."

Madora was such a universal favorite with all the slaves upon the plantation, that they could not bear the thoughts of her going away. She would often go around reading to them at night, and interesting them with her child-like talk.

Although Mrs. M—— knew that she was quite young to be sent from home, yet she thought it best that she should go. Besides, she did not know what might happen; she knew that misfortunes must come upon us all. Revolving these things in her mind, she decided positively to send her.

The winter was rapidly passing away, and, having much to put in readiness, she thought it advisable to commence immediately.

Fanny, whom Mrs. M—— had taught to sew very neatly, was quite busily engaged for some time; nothing afforded her more pleasure than to be doing something for Dora; she loved her so fondly, that she considered nothing a task which she did for her. With her assistance, and that of another sempstress, who

5

belonged to a Mr. B——, Mrs. M—— thought she would succeed in getting Dora ready in ample time.

The news of Dora's expected departure for school was soon spread over the plantation, and every one expressed their regret.

Aunt Nelly felt much grieved to part from her, for often Dora would go with her, on Sabbath evenings, to visit little Hannah's grave. Next to Hannah, in her affections, was Dora. She was the only one who could divert her mind from reflecting upon the loss of her child. She would talk so sweetly, and say that little Hannah was in heaven with the angels now.

One afternoon, Dora went with Aunt Nelly to visit the grave of Hannah; it was a bright and beautiful day, indeed; the sun was shining, and the little birds were singing. Never did the grave look more beautiful; the grass was beginning to come up, and just the green edges could be seen. Dora noticed that Aunt Nelly seemed silent for a long time, and asked her of what she was thinking.

"I was tinking, honey, dat yer was gwine away, and leab poor old Aunt Nelly; me won't hab no one to lub me den, nor come to dis grave wid me."

"Aunt Nelly, yes you will have some one to love you. Mamma loves you, for she told me so, and brother Charlie loves you too."

"But dat ain't like habing you wid me, for you is near to me almost as my Hannah; now she dead an' gone, you gwine to leab me, and den I won't hab nuffin' to lub."

"Won't you think of me, Aunt Nelly, when I am gone away? I shall always remember you."

"Oh! yes, dat I will; but, den, you will be so far away dat I can't see you; and when you comes back, poor old Aunt Nelly will be laying dar by dat blessed child. I'se gwine to tell missus to hab me put right dar; and when you comes back, Miss Dora, you must come and see my grave."

"Don't talk so, Aunt Nelly, you make me feel sad. I hope you won't be dead when I come back."

"Lors bless me, child, Aunt Nelly can't stand it much longer; and when de old ship ob Zion comes for me, den I must go. You see I'se been living dese many year, and when de angel is sent for me, I must leab missus, massa, and all. Den I will jine wid de angels den."

As Aunt Nelly spoke these words, tears streamed down her cheeks, for her feelings were wrought upon, being at the grave of her child, and then thinking of the parting with Dora. It would not be long before Dora would leave, for it was only a month before spring.

Aunt Nelly and Dora left the grave, to take a little ramble in the woods, and it was almost night before they got home.

Mrs. M—— questioned Dora as to where she had been.

"I have been to the grave of little Hannah, mamma, and you ought just to have heard poor old Aunt Nelly talk about Hannah, and about my going away. She does not want me to go, mamma; but I told her that when I come home I would be a large girl, and know so much more than I do now. She said she would have no one to love her now; and that, when I come, she would be dead."

"Well, my dear, you know Aunt Nelly is old now and she just thinks these things, as old people usually do; but she may live many years yet."

"I hope she will, mamma; but when am I going away?"

"In a little while, my dear; and I hope you will meet with many kind friends. If you conduct yourself properly, and observe the rules of the school, all the teachers will love you very much indeed; and if you are amiable and obliging to all of your schoolmates, they will be very fond of you, and your time will pass off very pleasantly."

"How long will I be gone, mamma, before I come home?"

"I don't know, my dear, exactly, how long; but, anyhow, I will come to see you very often, so do not be uneasy in the least, for you will be perfectly happy, I know. Just think, there will be so many little girls of your own age, who will be very kind to you, and will be glad to do anything for you."

"Yes, mamma, I think I will be very happy, indeed; and I know you will take good care of Aunt Phebe and Aunt Nelly while I am gone."

"Oh! certainly, my dear, I will see that they are properly attended to; you may rest perfectly contented about that."

Although Madora was twelve years of age, yet she was very childish, indeed; she had been such a pet of her parents, and also of the slaves. She had never gone to school much, as her delicate health would not permit. Her mother, being a highly educated lady, attended to her education herself. She was very apt, indeed, at learning anything, and bid fair to be a very intelligent woman.

Madora's health had improved so much, that she was getting to be quite a robust girl; and, with the advice of the physician, who thought the northern climate would be of service to her, she had no fears about sending her away.

As the time grew near for the departure of Madora, Mrs. M—— felt quite sad; she knew how much she would miss the society of Dora, and for a while could not divine how she would ever do without her. But she felt the importance of Madora's receiving a finished education, and she allowed that to gain the ascendency over her feelings.

Finding it necessary to pay a visit to the place where she intended sending Dora to school, she determined to write to her sister to come and take charge of her during her absence. She anticipated a visit from her anyhow, so she thought that the most auspicious time to send for her.

In about two weeks after her arrival, Mr. and Mrs. M—— left for R——; nor did she forget to give Madora particular injunctions to attend strictly to all her aunty said.

"I know she will do that," said Mrs. C——, at the same time kissing her beautiful white forehead. Little Dora put her fat arms around her neck, and promised to obey her sweet aunty, whom she so tenderly loved.

A week's journey brought Mrs. M—— to the place where Dora was to be educated. She entered a spacious mansion, where a group of young persons were seen, all appearing to be perfectly happy.

5*

It was a dark gray stone edifice, with four pillars in front, situated on quite a high eminence. In the spring-time it was beautifully shaded with trees, and flowers bloomed around. Mrs. M—— thought she had never seen a more beautiful spot in all her life. The garden was neatly laid out in grass plats, and the most choice flowers were planted there; on going down a hill, a sweet little arbor might be seen, on which the honey-suckle and woodbine crept in the summer. A stream of water rippled at the bottom of the hill, and a large cotton factory was at its brink.

The place appeared like a perfect Eden to Mrs. M——, and but for the fatigue of ascending the hill, she would have enjoyed the scenery very much. She thought it would be fine exercise for Dora to climb those hills, and knew that she would be delighted when she would tell her of the place.

She had been in the parlor but a few minutes, when Mrs. P—— was announced. She was delighted with her manners, and knew that she would be as kind to her as her open countenance indicated. Mrs. P—— had received a letter from Mrs. M——, stating that she intended sending her there to school, and that she would be there in the course of a week or two. So her arrival was not unexpected to Mrs. P——, for she had it in anticipation.

After examining the school, which Mrs. P—— kindly showed them, Mrs. M—— expressed the pleasure it afforded her to see how nicely everything appeared to go on, and then asked if she had any pupils there so young as twelve years.

"Oh! yes," replied Mrs. P——, "and many who are

much younger. I think it best to send them from home early, because they can learn so much better, for then their minds do not run upon beaux and such things, and they are apt to be more attentive to their studies. We never give them lessons which are too difficult, nor do we exact much from them while they are so young.

"Do you not put them under the charge of a teacher, who will see to them?"

"We always put them in the room with a teacher, who takes proper care of their clothing, and sees that they are well attended to. Miss B——, the vice-principal, has the younger pupils under her supervision, and they become very much attached to her. When do you design sending your daughter?"

"In about a month from now. I thought I had better wait until then, as it is quite cold here as yet; you do not have such an early spring here as we do South. Madora was in very bad health about two years ago, but is now quite the reverse. I think the trip to the Springs last summer was of great service to her. The doctor thought that a northern climate would agree with her."

"I shall be very happy to have your daughter here, and will see that she has every attention possible. If she is sick, I will let you know immediately, and will keep you advised of the progress she makes in her studies."

Mr. M—— observed to Mrs. P—— that he would like to stay a few days, to enjoy the beautiful scenery, but that business called him home, and he would have to leave that morning.

"I do wonder when mamma will come," said Dora to

her aunt one day; "it does seem to me that she has been gone a very long time. I am so anxious to hear of the school."

"It is your anxiety, my dear, which makes the time seem so long to you. I dare say she will be here in a day or two. I am in hopes so, at any rate; I am anxious to see her, and besides hear of your temporary home."

While they were talking, Dora heard Uncle Dick say, "Dar dey come; I told you so, ole ooman; I knowed massa would be here to-night."

Dora ran to the window, and, it being very bright moonlight, she could perceive the carriage coming.

"There they come, aunt Flora; oh! I am so glad, for we will hear about the beautiful place, where mamma intends sending me to school."

In a few minutes Mr. and Mrs. M—— entered; they both embraced Dora and her aunt; Dora could scarcely wait until her mamma had taken off her wrappings, before she begged her to tell her all about R——.

"Well, my dear, I have seen the place at last, and a charming spot it is; all around are trees and flowers, which are so beautiful in the spring."

With this description Dora was delighted, and put numerous questions to her mother.

"Did you see many little girls like me, mamma?"

"Oh, yes, my dear, a number of them, and they all looked very happy, and I thought if you were there how you would enjoy yourself!"

"Mamma, I am so anxious to go; when will I go?"

"Very soon, my dear!"

Charles had been absent about a week at his uncle's, a much loved and only brother of Mr. M——. He had not as yet returned, but he was notified of Dora's intended departure by his aunt, and so he, of course, would make all haste to return home. He had expressed his desire to go to college in his letter to Dora.

"Mamma, Charlie says that he wants to go to college too!"

"Your papa intends sending him soon; we would have sought out a place for him while we were away, but we could not make it convenient to stay any longer."

"I do wish he would hurry home so that I could tell him, for I know he would be delighted!"

It is not to be wondered at that Dora was so much pleased with the idea of going away to school, as it was something novel for her; and, besides, what did she know about a boarding-school? She pictured in imagination a group of young children like herself, and thought of the pleasure she would see in their company. She had heard her mother speak of the high hills over which she would roam, and the lovely flowers which bloomed there.

The sister of Mrs. M—— had come to spend some time with her, and she, of course, assisted much in preparing Dora for school. Each day she would review her in her studies, and was very careful that she understood everything she learned. Mrs. C——, like her sister, had been thoroughly educated at one of the first seminaries. Their father was an extremely intellectual gentleman, and highly appreciated a good mind; so the first step he took with his daughters was to see that their minds were properly cultivated. Consequently, they were sent to a large boarding-school at an early age, and remained until they had completed their course

of study. They had not been from school more than
twelve months before they married very wealthy planters,
Mr. M—— and Mr. C——. Their father settled a large
estate upon his daughters after their marriage, and that,
united with the wealth of the planters, afforded means
to live in the most luxuriant manner possible. They
had never a want from their infancy, for they had, indeed, been reared in opulence.

The first grief, since the death of her mother, which
Mrs. C—— had known, was the loss of her husband.
But troubles do not come alone, as the poet says, for
they tread upon the heels of each other.

Her husband had been dead but a few weeks when
her only child was taken ill and died. She now felt
that all she loved was gone, and, amid all that opulence,
she could not be happy, because the one who once shared
it with her had been called from time to eternity.

Mrs. M—— had written to her many times, request-
ing her to make her a visit, but she could not make it
convenient to accept the invitation until now, and it
happened at a very favorable season, too, for Mrs.
M—— had not time to review Madora in her studies
prior to her leaving for boarding-school. Every minute,
almost, was employed in getting the wardrobe of Dora
arranged, and she felt as though no one could do it so
well as herself. Besides all this, the thoughts of parting with her only daughter grieved her so much that
she did not feel able to pay that strict attention to her
studies that would be required.

Busy in making preparations for Dora's departure,
we leave them for the present, and will describe her
leaving for school in another chapter.

CHAPTER V.

THE SURPRISE WEDDING.

RUFUS became more and more attached to Laura; ever since the night on which they danced together, he could think of nothing else but his "lubly Laura." Every moment that they were at leisure was spent in the society of each other; and, at last, he thought he would muster up courage enough to ask her to have him. But how in the world he was to go about it, he did not know. He was not much versed in courting matters, anyhow; indeed, he was so fickle, as Aunt Phebe used to say, "dat she neber did b'lieve he would ax' anybody to hab him."

One Sunday evening, he went for Laura to take a walk. He felt as though his tongue was tied, he found it such a difficulty to speak.

He, however, after awhile, commenced in his flattering way, as usual, which sounded like music in the ears of Laura, for she never once dreamed what flattery was. She always took him at his word, no matter what it was he said.

"You look lubly, dis ebening; your eyes shines like dat black cat of our'n in de night. Lors bless me, if you ain't de purtiest gal I eber did see, I'll gib up!"

"Lah! you will make me wain if you talks dat way; you allays told me dat I was purty, but I'se afeard you will spile me by tellin' me on it so often."

"Oh! oh! oh! my heart, my heart!"

"Why, what's de matter, Rufus?" said Laura, much frightened.

"I'se got a pain in dis 'ere heart, Laura!"

"Ain't dar nuffin' yer can take to aise it?"

"Lors bless me, why, yes, Laura."

"Do tell me what it is, so that we can hurry home and get it."

"Just one word from you, Laura, will cure me."

"What word is it?"

"Yes."

"Well, yes, then."

"What, will yer agree to hab me, den?" asked Rufus, much delighted.

"You must be foolish, Rufus; you don't want me for sure."

Rufus now gave free vent to his feelings. "My lubly Laura, I lubs you more den I do de best pie Aunt Phebe makes; and if you will only hab me, den we can hab a weddin' right off, and we will git Ben to play de banjo for us."

The thoughts of dancing somewhat elevated Laura's spirits, who agreed to give Rufus her hand and heart.

Rufus appointed an early time for the wedding to come off, for he was so fickle-minded, that he was afraid he might get out of the notion if he did not hurry.

Evening was coming upon them rapidly, so they hastened home from their walk, for Rufus had the tea-table to arrange, and he knew that when they got home it would be tea-time.

He could scarcely wait to set the table, before he went

to Aunt Phebe's cabin to tell her what had transpired between Laura and himself.

He got around in some way, by letting Aunt Phebe know that he wanted his best white vest and pants put in fine order by the next Saturday night two weeks.

"What on airth does yer want wid dat west dis time ob de yar?—yer had better keep it till de summer, I tell yer."

"Aunt Phebe, I habs somefing to tell you, but you mustn't tell for de world."

Aunt Phebe was much pleased with confidence, with which she was intrusted, and told him that she "would neber tell anybody, not eben her ole man."

"Do tell me what it be, for I wants to know; you needn't be afeard dat I mention it 'gin, for I don't talk nohow, but tings what folks tells me."

"Well, Aunt Phebe," said Rufus, bringing a broad grin, "I'se gwine to be married!"

"Gwine to be married, Rufus! Lors a massy, who to?"

"Why de most perfectionist Laura."

"Well, well; dat ar' beats all I eber heerd tell ob. I don't b'lieve it, nohow; 'caze I know how fickle yer is, too well."

"Now don't say one word 'bout it, Aunt Phebe, 'caze I wants to s'prise dem all wid de weddin'. I won't gib em de invitations till de day afore. I'se gwine to axe massa to-night; and I'se gwine to tell her not to say nuffin' 'bout it."

Mrs. M—— had finished tea, and was reading, when

6

she heard a rap at the door. She was sitting there alone, for Madora and her aunt had gone up stairs.

"Who is there?" asked Mrs. M——.

"Me, missus."

"You, Rufus?"

"Yes, marm, missus."

"Well, come in."

"Missus, I comed here to axe yer, if yer had any 'jections to habbing a weddin' at de plantation?"

"A wedding, Rufus?" said Mrs. M——, much surprised; "and, pray, who is going to be married?"

"Me, missus."

"You, Rufus!" and Mrs. M—— laughed heartily.

"Yes, marm," replied Rufus, hiding his face and tittering at a great rate.

"Who is to be the bride?" (Mrs. M—— suspected Laura all the time.)

"Laura, marm."

"Well, Rufus, I have no objections to your marrying any one you wish; and if you think you are capable of taking care of a wife, I will consent. You must remember that this is a matter which is not to be decided upon hastily; and if you think the love is mutual, I am perfectly willing."

"Tank you, marm, missus; and dat is all I hab to say, 'cepts one more word."

"What is that, Rufus?"

"Missus, please marm, don't say nuffin' 'bout it, 'caze I wants to s'prise all de niggers; dey don't know one word 'bout it."

"Very well, Rufus, I won't mention it, only to your master."

" Good-ebening, missus."

" Good-night, Rufus ; send Laura to me ; I wish to speak to her."

" Yes, marm, I will, dis berry minute."

Away Rufus ran to tell Laura that her mistress had consented, and that she wished to see her.

One can imagine Laura's agitation, for she was rather bashful, anyhow; and she said that she did not know how she was " eber gwine to stand dat."

In a few minutes Laura made her appearance, as smiling as a May morning.

Mrs. M——, as usual, met Laura with a smile. " I hear, Laura," said she, " that you are to be married very soon, and I was quite surprised to hear it. I suspected that something of the kind was going on, but could not decide certainly. It is a very important step which you are about to take, Laura, and I hope that you are not going to act unadvisedly. I have no objections in the world to your marrying Rufus, and will gladly get anything that you may want."

"I tank yer, marm, missus. You has been mighty good to me, and I will always tank you for it. I thought it best dat Rufus should speak to you 'rectly 'bout it, 'caze I knew dat you oughter know it fuss."

" Yes, he did very right, Laura, in informing me of the fact so soon, and I will be enabled to get anything in readiness. I suppose you would like to have your white dress fixed?"

" Yes, marm, missus, if you pleases!"

" Bring it to me to-morrow, Laura, and I will have it done for you. Have you not something else you would like arranged ? If there is any furniture you wish, I will get it for you, as I expect to go to town to-morrow. I shall also get you two handsome bridal-cakes, and other things which will be requisite."

Laura thanked her mistress very much, and named over some little things she would like to have to set off her cabin, and then bade her a good-evening, and promised to bring the dress the following morning.

Rufus waited down at the door until Laura should come out. He was all eagerness to hear what her mistress had to say, and when she told him that she promised to bring some furniture, he was highly delighted.

"Dat ar' missus, if she ain't de best ooman I eber seed in all my life. What, me leab her? No! no! dis nigger's gwine to stay wid her long as she will hab him!"

The couple went to Aunt Phebe's cabin and found her sitting there all alone. Uncle Dick was paying a visit to some of the cabins, and the children were fast asleep.

Aunt Phebe, seeing them coming, was not a little delighted, for she was as much interested in the wedding as any one. She was always ready to give advice where she thought it was needed, and now she thought it a very favorable opportunity of offering some.

"Well, chil'en, as yer are all alone now wid me, I tinks it my duty to gib yer a little adwice. Yer knows dat Phebe's quite old now, and knows more 'bout de world dan yer does. Yer is gwine to take a mighty 'sponsible step, an' I hopes, arter all, it will turn out for de best. Nuffin' pleases me more dan to see yer both happy, and I hopes yer will neber hab no trouble. Phebe will do all she can for yer, an', if missus say so, I will make yer a plenty of nice cakes; she is sich a blessed good ooman, so kind to her sarvants,. dat I know she will hab ebery ting in de fust style. Dar comes ole man; I s'pose yer don't want him to know it nohow, 'caze yer wants to s'prise him as well as de rest."

"Hush! hush! Aunt Phebe," said Rufus; "he will hear you."

Uncle Dick entered.

"I say, ole ooman, how yer all been musin' yerselfs eber since I been gone? I tought I would jist step round and see how Aunt Nelly was."

"Well, how did you find her, ole man?"

"Not in berry good spirits; she is sorter 'jected, I tink, 'bout Miss Dora's gwine way. She say how she lubs her next to Hannah. I'se mighty sorry for her, but de good Being does all tings for de best. You looks mighty smilin' to-night, Laura; what am de matter? I neber seed you look better in my life."

Rufus said not a word, but looked at Aunt Phebe sideways, and gave Laura an occasional wink, who could scarcely keep from tittering in spite of herself, for she tried to look very demure on the occasion.

"I had a mighty strange dream 'bout you, Rufus, last night, an' I don't know what to make ob it, for 'taint often dat I dream nohow, and, when I do, I tinks it must mean somefing."

"What was it, Uncle Dick?"

"Why, I tought you was gwine to be married to some spruce young gal; but I don't recollect who it was."

"What a strange dream!" said Rufus, at the same time giving Aunt Phebe a touch at the elbow; "folks

will hab mighty strange dreams sometimes, Uncle Dick,
you know."

"It did seem mighty funny dat I should be dreaming
'bout you, 'caze I wa'n't tinking 'bout you, nohow!"

Rufus did not seem disposed to dwell upon the subject
any longer, so he just made a turning point by asking
uncle how his "rheumatiz was getting on nowadays, for
he neber heerd him 'plaining now."

"Oh! I'se getting much better, tank yer, Rufus, and
I'se mighty glad dat winter is so far gone, for I feels
better in de spring and summer; dese here keen nights,
which we hab sometimes, sorter makes my poor ole bones
ache!"

The conversation now being pretty much exhausted,
they separated, after calling Aunt Phebe aside to tell
her to be sure "and not mention 'bout de weddin' to
Uncle Dick, for den de fun would all be spiled."

As might be expected, Laura was very busy making
all preparations for the great occasion. Mrs. M——
told her that she might have those two weeks to herself
to prepare whatever she wished, at the same time offering all assistance. Her white dress was neatly repaired,
and then nicely washed by Aunt Phebe, who took a
great deal of pains.

Mrs. M—— had made quite a number of purchases
for Laura; among the number were some ornaments for
the hair, white kid gloves, and a very fine handkerchief
neatly worked.

Laura viewed all these things with delight, and was
on the eve of telling Rufus, but thought she would

rather surprise him by fixing up very smartly for the wedding.

Nor did Mrs. M—— forget Rufus; she had bought him a nice pair of pumps, and a very pretty neck-tie, and a neat cambric handkerchief.

Rufus could think of nothing else but the wedding; he left his work undone at times, but Mr. M—— did not censure him, for he well knew that his attention was so wholly engrossed with the thoughts of his "lubly Laura," that he could think of nothing else.

Rufus and Laura showed the wedding apparel which Mrs. M—— had bought for them, who said that " de niggers would star' dat night, anyhow."

Rufus was so delighted with his pumps that he had to put them on, and shuffle about the floor, to see how he could dance in them. Aunt Phebe, who had been watching him all the time, told him that he "had better take dem ar' boots off, if he didn't want to scrape 'em all out afore de marriage."

Two weeks were passing very rapidly, and began to draw to a close. The cakes were all in readiness, and Mrs. M—— had some very nice jelly and other sweetmeats taken from her pantry for the occasion.

One day Mrs. M—— called Rufus to her, and said that he had better give the invitations out, as it was now only three days before the wedding, and they might all wish to put their clothes in readiness.

So off started Rufus, to invite them. The first person he hailed was Ben, who was practising on his banjo. The sight of this pleased Rufus, for he thought of the dance they would have.

"I say, Ben, don't yer want to go to a veddin' ?"

Ben looks up, much surprised: "A weddin'! yes, I guess I does; who's gwine to get married, and when is de weddin' comin' off?" Ben's eyes began to brighten up, for he now thought of what a fine opportunity he would have to show off the last piece which he had learned on the banjo. "I say, Rufus, who's gwine to get married?"

"Why, de berry nigger what yer see standin' fore yer now."

"Yer don't say so."

"It is really true."

"Who to, Rufus?"

"Laura. Oh! it does dis here nigger good to call dat ar' name, it habs so much music in de word. She am sweeter dan de biggest hogshead of 'lasses dat massa eber bought."

"When is it gwine to be?"

"Next Saturday night, sartin, and a nice time we ar' gwine to hab, for missus fotched me the most beautiful pumps you eber see; an' won't dis nigger dance? Yer will play for us, Ben?"

"Oh, sartinly, wid all my heart; and won't I make de banjo ring? I will dat."

Rufus, who felt a little too bashful to go all around the plantations, giving the invitations, thought he would get Ben to do so.

"I hab a favor to ax of yer, Ben; will yer grant it?"

"Sartinly, anything; what is it?"

"Why, jist go round and gib all de niggers on de plantations an invitation to de weddin'."

Ben, who was much delighted to have this news to

spread abroad, readily consented, and in a few minutes was off.

"Well, I declare how dey has s'prised us," all exclaimed. "What, dat ar' foolish nigger Rufus gwine to be married ? Well, I'se glad to go, I tell yer. Did eber yer see anything kept so still in all yer life ? Dey tells me dat all de cakes is made, and put away. Well, if dat don't beat all I eber seed in my life. Dis is a real s'prise to us all, I tell yer it is."

Uncle Dick said that "ole ooman mought hab told him 'fore dis, 'caze she knowed all about it." He was as much surprised as the rest, at the unexpected news.

"I tink, ole ooman, yer might hab told me 'bout dis ar' 'fair."

"Yer didn't tink I was gwine to 'tray de secret what Rufus told me. No, cotch dis ar' nigger doin' dat ar' sort ob ting. Why, don't yer see dat she was up to s'prisin' yer ?"

"Dese ar' niggers, ole ooman, is up to ebery ting. I tink it's time de cakes war' makin'. I 'spects missus gwine to hab ebery ting mighty nice."

"Why, lors bless me, ole man ; I'se done made 'em two days ago."

"Vel, I tought you was makin' a mighty heap ob dem, but den, tinks I, massa gwine to hab some ob de great gemmen here, so I axed no questions 'bout it. I declar', if all dem ar' nice cakes ain't for dat ar' nigger's weddin'; he hab got a mighty good missus, I tell you, and I 'spects dat de supper dey will hab is gwine to make dem kill demselves eatin'; vel, vel, dis here nigger is up to ebery ting in de world, I does belie've. A tought has just struck me, ole ooman ; dat is what you was so busy

'bout washing dem ar' white pants and west ob Rufus;
dat's what dem ar' pumps are for ; wonder ole Uncle
Dick couldn't see better dan dat; neber mind, I'll be
up to 'em de next time, I will."

While Uncle Dick was talking, Aunt Phebe was busy
ironing Laura's white dress.

" I s'pose dat's de dress, is it, dat she's gwine to git
married in ?"

" Yes, dis is it, and don't it look purty ?" said Aunt
Phebe, holding it up, and viewing it with much satisfaction. " I s'pects she will shine dat night, for missus
hab got a mighty heap ob purty tings for her to war ;
you jist oughter hab seen 'em; neber mind, you will see
'em Saturday."

Uncle Dick sat for some time silent, thinking of
the wedding, and of the surprise with which he had met,
while Aunt Phebe went singing away, ironing the dress
which was to be worn on that wonderful occasion.

When the news of Rufus's intended marriage was
spread over the plantation (which flew like wildfire),
every one had his own opinion to express about it.

" I say, Ben, what does yer tink ob dis matter, anyhow ?"

" Vel, Mike, I don't know; for yer see dat ar' nigger
Rufus ain't got no sense nohow, 'tall, and I s'pects he
won't make much on it, 'caze yer see, he is so fickle dat
I dono how to trus' him. Did yer hear how he treated
dat ar' gal ob Mr. Tomkins's ?"

" No; what am it ?"

" He went courtin' on de gal, an' she was habing de
weddin' clothes made up, an' den he backed out. Dat

ar' beats all I eber heard ob in all my life. I s'pects he will serve Laura dat ar' way too, if she don't mind."

"No, I tink he won't, Miky, 'caze dis be Wednesday, an' he is gwine to hab de ceremony on Saturday night."

"Any dancin', Ben?"

"Egad, and dar is; an' ain't I gwine to make dat ar' ole banjo ob mine ring den? I tell you what, dem dar niggers will tink dat dey neber seed de like afore. I don't s'pects dat dar will be much work done on dis here plantation dis week. Massa done tole Rufus dat if he had preparations to make, dat he would 'scuse him."

The long looked for night came! What a commotion there was upon the plantation; every one was trying to see who could look the best; consequently there was quite a time among the slaves.

Laura was dressing in the house; her mistress was anxious to fix her herself, so she told her to bring in her dressing, and she would assist her in making her toilet.

She placed white roses on either side of her hair, which contrasted strongly with its ebon hue. Laura prided herself upon her hair, for it was very long and glossy, such as the creoles have.

After Mrs. M—— had arranged her hair, Laura was very anxious to see how it looked; so she walked up to the glass, and it was evident from her smile that she thought she looked charming, and thought of what Rufus would say when he saw her.

Soon the white dress and sash were put on—then came the white kid gloves; she now looked very much like a bride indeed. A pretty bouquet, which Mrs.

M—— had culled from the conservatory, consisting of white roses prettily mixed with geranium leaves, was presented to her by her mistress.

Rufus, too, looked as bright as a new brass button. His collar was stiff and white; the neck-tie, which Mrs. M—— had given him, was arranged with considerable taste; his boots shone like glass, and his white kid gloves occupied quite a conspicuous position.

He was waiting below until Laura should complete her toilet, and the time for the ceremony to commence. Mrs. M—— had a large spare room which she had nicely fixed up for the occasion.

The toilet being completed, and the parson having arrived, Laura came down, and now they all enter the room. Ben stood with his collar high and stiff enough to cut his throat, while the banjo was lying on the table in readiness.

The ceremony being over, Mr. and Mrs. M—— retired, to give them a fair opportunity for enjoying themselves.

They all thought that Rufus and Laura looked very handsome. The bride (as she expected) received a shower of compliments, much to her own gratification and of Rufus.

Aunt Phebe and Uncle Dick had quite an air of importance that evening, and seemed to be the head ones there.

In a few minutes the banjo struck up, which was a signal for the dancing to commence; soon every one was on his feet and ready.

Laura and Rufus took the head of the cotillon, and every eye was turned towards them. Such a shuffling of feet was never heard before; they fairly made the whole house quake. Mrs. M—— was delighted to find that they were all enjoying themselves so much, for nothing afforded her more pleasure than to see her servants happy.

In the dining-room a large table was set, on which everything in the way of edibles was placed. The bridal cakes were iced, and beautifully ornamented; Mrs. M—— had spared no pains in getting everything as nice as possible. After they had danced awhile, they went into the supper-room—Aunt Phebe at the head of the table, and Uncle Dick at the foot, while Aunt Nelly stood on the side. The bride received all attention possible. Ben was bowing and scraping at a great rate, very politely waiting upon her, at the same time spicing it in with compliments, which were not at all unpleasant to Laura.

The evening passed off very agreeably indeed, and they agreed in saying that the night of Rufus's marriage would be long remembered by all on the plantation. They often expressed a desire to meet with just such another surprise as that of Rufus's marriage.

CHAPTER VI.

MADORA'S DEPARTURE FOR SCHOOL.

THE winter glided rapidly away. Spring came in all her beauty; the birds were singing gayly; the flowers around were blooming. In a word, everything had a charming aspect.

The day for Dora's departure arrived—a sad one, indeed, for Mrs. M——. Dora had never left her before for more than a week or so, in her life; and now the thought that she must go so far away from her grieved her sadly. Yet, at the same time, she knew that Dora must be educated, and there was no alternative but to send her away for awhile.

"Well, my dear," said Mrs. M—— to Dora, the day on which she was to leave, "we must part to-day; this afternoon your father will start with you for boarding-school. I sincerely hope that you will be ever happy, and that you will become attached to the instructors and pupils. Mrs. P—— seems to be a very fine lady, and I know you will love her. You must not expect to find all things there as you do at home, and have a servant to wait upon you on all occasions. At the North, you know, there are no slaves, as there are here, and you must do the best you can."

"Don't they have any servants, mamma?"

"Yes, my dear, but they are white, or else free colored people. But you know that at boarding-school you cannot expect to have everything as you do at home, for there are many to be waited upon besides yourself."

"I know that I shall be very happy indeed. I will see so many little girls like myself, and I know I will love them."

"I hope so, my dear ; you must be very kind and obliging to them, and they will love you the more for it."

As they were to leave that afternoon, dinner was prepared much earlier, so that they would not be at all hurried in getting off. While Dora and her mother were talking, the dinner-bell rang, and they assembled in the dining-room.

Charles, hearing that his sister would leave home so soon, hastened to get there before she should start. Seeing his sister getting off, put him in a greater notion than ever for going away, and he determined to persuade his papa to send him soon to college. But it would not require much persuasion, for Mr. M—— had fully intended sending him.

Dinner being over, Dora went around to all the cabins to bid them "goodby." Aunt Nelly cried almost as much as when little Hannah died, and said that she " neber 'spected to see Miss Dora agin in dis world, for when she come back, she would be in de grave." She took little Dora in her arms, and caressed her, and told her " not to forget poor old Aunt Nelly, and if she neber seed her 'gin on airth, she hoped to meet her in heaben." The next cabin she went to was Aunt Phebe's. Uncle Dick knew that she was

going away, so he stayed expressly to see her. He and
Aunt Phebe said that they were "mighty sorry dat Miss
Dora was gwine away." Old Aunt Phebe wept, and
said, "Miss Dora, don't forget poor old Aunt Phebe;"
and Uncle Dick, "Don't let dem Norrud folks 'suade
you in none ob dar notions." Tears fell from the eyes
of both Aunt Phebe and Uncle Dick, as they bade her
adieu. "De Lord bless yer," fell from the lips of
each, and Dora, after wishing them much happiness,
left the cabin. How like a fairy spirit did her form
disappear from their view, and, as her golden curls
kissed the passing breeze, she had the appearance of an
angel more than anything else.

As she was going around to the other cabins, she met
Ben, with his banjo. "I heerd dem say, Miss Dora, dat
yer was gwine away to-day, and I tought how I would
jist play one little tune for yer ; if yer has no 'jections,
I will do so."

"Thank you, Ben; I want you to play your best."

With this Ben struck up, and played away at a great
rate, and would have played a much longer time, but he
knew that his young mistress had to pay a visit to some
of the other cabins.

"I want yer to tell dem dar Norrud folks, Miss Dora,
how dis nigger can play de banjo; tell 'em dat he is
hard to beat, and dat if dey will only come down dis
way, Ben will show 'em what it am to make de banjo
sound."

It is not necessary to describe severally the parting
of Dora with the slaves. Suffice it to say, that they all
expressed deep regret, and said that " the life of the

plantation would be gone sure enough, for Massa Charles was gwine too."

The most important and affecting parting was that of Dora with her mother. It was as if some one had touched the very strings of her heart. But she knew that she must—must yield; so, with many affectionate kisses, she turned from Dora, who was now helped into the carriage, and in a few minutes she was out of sight.

The scenes in travelling were entirely new to Dora; they interested her much, and caused the ride to appear less monotonous than it would otherwise have been.

"When will we get there, papa?"

"Not for a week, my dear."

Dora was delighted at the idea of a week's travelling, although she was quite anxious to see the school. It is pleasant travelling in the spring; when the weather becomes settled everything appears so beautiful, and the air is so balmy; the fields are fragrant with perfumes of flowers, and the song of birds greets our ear; the skies are clear and blue, and nature awakens, as it were, from her dormant state, and now rejoices.

During their journey they met with many persons travelling, and Dora became quite a favorite. She was particularly interesting in her conversation and manners, and withal very observing, as was evident from the many questions which she asked her father.

One day, towards the close of her journey, she became a little fatigued, and said, "Papa, I am very tired; when will we get there?"

"Very soon, my dear; we are not more than six miles off."

"I am delighted to hear it."

Her father, to make the time seem shorter, began to talk about the flowers, and how beautiful the place was, and what delightful rambles she would have over the hills.

In a few minutes a great roaring was heard; it sounded so strange to Dora.

"What is that, papa?"

"It is the noise of the factory, my dear, and in a very few minutes we will be there."

Sure enough, it was a very few minutes indeed. The large mansion now peered from amid the trees, and she saw a number of little girls skipping about, the size of herself.

"See, see, papa, how many little girls, just like myself. They all appear so merry, and I know I will be happy there."

They now commenced ascending the hill, which caused Dora to be quite fatigued, not having been used to any but level ground.

"I am very tired, papa," said Dora, as she seated herself upon a rock to rest.

"You will soon get used to this. See how the little girls are skipping about, like so many lambs; they do not appear to mind it, and I expect, the next time I come, I will see you running over these hills as they are now doing. If you have rested, Dora, we will go up to the house now."

Dora jumped up in a minute, and bounded away for life.

"Why, I see you are improving already, Dora. I am

thinking you will make rapid progress. Here we are, now.''

Mr. M—— and his daughter entered the spacious mansion, and in a short time were received by Mrs. P——, the lady of whom Dora had heard so much.

Dora was equally as delighted as her mother was with Mrs. P——, and when she addressed her in such a mild manner, she liked her still more.

"So you are the little girl," said Mrs. P——, "who has come to live with me awhile. I dare say we shall get along very nicely, and you will be much pleased after you have become acquainted. I have a great many little girls here, some much younger than yourself, and have come from as great a distance. What is your given name, my dear?"

"Madora."

"That is a very pretty name, and a very short one, too. In a few days you will be perfectly delighted with the school, for you will feel more at home, and will form a great many acquaintances."

Mr. M—— had some business to attend to North, so he was compelled to leave that evening, much to the regret of Mrs. P——, who desired that he should remain longer.

He bade Dora adieu, and told her that she must obey all that the instructors told her, and must write home often.

Mrs. P—— promised that she would see that she wrote home once a week, at least.

"Her mother," said Mr. M——, "is much grieved at parting with her, and will not be satisfied until she hears how she is pleased; so I would like to have her write home about to-morrow, and inform her mother of her arrival, and how she likes the place. They say that first impressions are generally the most lasting; hers are indeed favorable, and I would like to have her write soon."

After Mr. M—— had left, Mrs. P—— sent for one of the little girls with whom Dora would room, in order to introduce her. She called her Fanny Wilding.

It seems that Fanny was quite struck with the appearance of Dora, and they ran off into the arbor to play.

Those who have been to a boarding-school know what a sensation a new scholar produces, and how many questions are asked about her. When Dora entered the room, every eye was turned towards her.

" Who is that ?" asked one.

" Isn't she pretty ?" said another.

" It is a new scholar," said a third.

" It is my room-mate," said a fourth.

After tea, the little girls all flocked around her, and seemed to take a fancy to her, so that soon she became acquainted with a number of the girls.

She was sent for by one of the teachers under whose care she was placed, and in a few minutes was in her presence.

"What is your name ?" said she, brushing her hair from her brow.

" Madora; but mamma and Aunt Phebe call me Dora."

"Madora, then, is your name. I think we shall be very good friends; I have three other little girls with me, and we will all have a merry time. You are a little Southerner, I believe?"

"Yes, ma'am. I think it is colder here than it was there."

"Yes, my dear, we always have it colder North than you do South. Have you ever been North before?"

"Only a little while, in the summer."

"I think you will be much pleased, and, after you have been here some time, you will have bright roses on your cheeks. Who is Aunt Phebe, my dear?"

Dora looked up, a little surprised to think that she did not know who Aunt Phebe was, for she thought every one must know her.

"It is my nurse; and she is so good to me, and nursed me when I was a little baby. I love her and Aunt Nelly too; they cried so much when I left them, and said I must not stay away too long from them."

Miss B—— knew, from Dora's manner of speaking, that she was a very innocent child, and had a very tender heart. She suspected who Aunt Phebe was, but thought she would question her upon that subject, as it would be likely to interest her.

The study-bell rang, and Dora asked what bell that was.

"It is the study-bell, my dear, and when that rings, all of the girls study their lessons for to-morrow. Little girls like you do not have to study long, like the larger ones. You are fatigued, my dear, after travelling so long, and I think you had better retire now."

It sounded quite strange to Dora for any one to say that she was allowed to retire, for at home she always used her own pleasure about that. But she remem-

bered what her mother had told her, that she must not
expect to find everything at boarding-school as she
did at home.

In a few minutes after the study-bell rang, all the
girls were quietly seated, and commenced to study their
lessons. Dora noticed the order which was observed,
and began to think she would like the school very much,
for no one seemed to infringe upon the rights of others.

Dora retired, as Miss B—— had desired her to do, as
she knew she must be fatigued from travelling. Indeed,
her looks indicated it to be the case.

She slept very sweetly that night, and dreamed of
her home. Again she saw Aunt Phebe and Aunt Nelly,
and talked with them. She dreamed, too, of seeing
little Hannah's grave, and thought the jasmine,
which Uncle Dick had planted there, never looked
more beautiful than it did then.

The next morning she was awakened by the ringing
of a large bell. She got up, and was to commence that
day, as it were, a new life.

Mrs. P—— sent for Dora that morning, to question
her respecting her studies, and classed her.

"How are you pleased with the school, so far, Dora,
and how do you like your room-mates?"

"Oh! I like them very much indeed. Miss B——
is so kind to us, and I like all the girls, too. Last night
Miss B—— let me go to bed quite early, for I was very
tired indeed."

"Do you think you can be satisfied to stay away from
your ma, awhile?"

"Yes, ma'am, I think I will be contented, and not
get homesick."

"I am very glad to hear that you are so much pleased. As you have no lessons to recite to-day, I think you had better write to your mother, and tell her all about your arrival here, and how you are pleased with the school, for I know she is very anxious to hear all about you. You can go now into the school-room, and write to your mamma."

Dora was now about to do something which was entirely new to her—that of writing to her mother. She had never in her life been separated from her more than a week. The idea of writing to her pleased her very much indeed. So down she sat, to fulfil the important commission of Mrs. P——.

She gave a description of the place, and how much delighted she was with the teachers and girls. She told her of the rambles she had over the hills, after school hours, and it did not tire her so much to ascend them as it did at first. She did not fail to speak of the kindness of Miss B—— and Mrs. P——. Aunt Phebe and Aunt Nelly were mentioned, and she sent her best love to both, and told her mamma to tell Aunt Phebe that Miss B—— said she would have roses on her cheeks when she came home.

The letter showed Mrs. M—— that Dora was delighted with her new home, and the acquaintances she had formed.

Mrs. M—— did not expect a letter from Dora so soon, and when Rufus brought it to her, she was so much delighted that she could not break the seal fast enough. A mother who has parted for the first time with an only daughter can imagine the feelings of Mrs. M—— on the reception of Dora's letter. She felt happy to think that she was so much delighted, and so happy, and hoped that nothing would interfere to destroy the felicity.

Aunt Phebe and Aunt Nelly, hearing from Rufus that Mrs. M—— had received a letter from Miss Dora, now went in full speed to hear the news. Aunt Phebe almost cried with joy when she heard her mention her name, and as great an effect was produced upon Aunt Nelly. "De Lors bless dat child; if she ain't an angel; see how she recollects us, and den sends her best love." "I hope," said Aunt Nelly, "dat I will lib to see her 'gin, but somehow I tink I be trabelling home afore dat time."

Uncle Dick was sitting at the cabin door, anxiously waiting for Aunt Phebe to come and tell him the news. "Well, ole ooman, what did she say?"

"Oh! she is mighty pleased, and say dat all de folks is kind to her, and when she comes home she will hab roses on her cheeks."

"I am glad on dat, for she was pale 'nuff when she went 'way from here."

"I knowed dat de folks would be kind to her, for any body would to dat sweet child, dat dey would."

"When massa comin' home?"

"Vel, she didn't say, but I 'spects he will be 'long here in a day or two. You know massa went Norf on some business."

As might be expected, Aunt Phebe had quite a crowd around her to hear the news, for Rufus had told them all that a letter had been received from his young mistress.

Mrs. M—— was in much better spirits after the reception of Dora's letter, and felt that she ought to be very thankful that Dora was so contented and happy. Now, again reading over the letter which she had so gladly received that morning, we will let her enjoy its contents, and hope that Dora will ever remain thus satisfied with her new home.

CHAPTER VII.

MR. I——'S DESCRIPTION OF HIS VISIT SOUTH.

WHEN we last spoke of Mr. I——, he was at the inn, resting himself from the fatigue of his journey. He remained there but one night, being anxious to make his way home. Mrs. I—— had been expecting him daily, and could not account for his prolonged stay.

He arrived home in about two weeks after we left him at the inn, having met with many detentions on the road, from various causes. He was really glad to get to the end of his journey, for he was heartily tired of travelling.

After he had been home a day or two, Mrs. I—— questioned him respecting his visit South.

"Well, how were you pleased with the South, and how did you pass your time among the slave-holders?"

"Do not speak so lightly," said Mr. I——; "I never in all my life met with better treatment. Really, if you want to have an idea of genuine hospitality, just go to the South, and you will find it. I never in my life met with a more cordial reception, and by a stranger, too!"

"I shall begin to think you have turned a Southerner in notions. I expect you will get to be an advocate for slavery, next."

"Not by any means. But listen to me while I tell

you of the hospitality with which I met at the South. A gentleman by the name of M—— happened to fall in with me in travelling, and he saw how much fatigued I was, and knowing that there was no inn near, he kindly invited me to remain with him that night, and extended his invitation to some days. His wife is a perfect lady, in every sense of the word. She treated me as kindly as possible, and more kind and affable manners I have never met with in all my life. It seems to me that she had a smile for every one."

" I am glad to hear that you were treated so kindly, and heartily thank Mrs. M——. But what did you think of the slaves, down South ?"

" I must say, that I verily believe they all appeared to be perfectly happy ; they were singing when they were at work, and they seem to like their owners very much indeed. I had a conversation with one, who told me that he did not desire his freedom."

" He must like his situation better than I should," replied Mrs. I——.

" You cannot imagine how contented they are, and what care their owners take of them. Why should they desire to change their situation ? They cannot better themselves; probably they would not be as well off."

Mrs. I—— seemed much surprised at the answer her husband made, and said that she believed he would turn slave-holder himself.

Mr. I—— replied by saying that he was only speaking from what he had seen, and knew to be the truth, and that if she had been there she would have had the same opinion as himself.

" No, you can never make me believe that the slaves are happy South, they have so much hard labor to perform ; and then the knowledge that they are slaves, is enough to make them unhappy."

"I do not suppose they ever reflect upon such a thing," said Mr. I——. "The Northerners are laboring under a very mistaken impression, as regards the manner in which the slaves are treated South. They think they receive nothing but cruel treatment from their owners. It is exactly the contrary ; for I know that they would never look so bright and cheerful if they were cruelly treated, as many of the Northerners assert."

" I am almost sorry that you ever went South, as you have brought back such ideas with you."

" You would have just the very same if you had witnessed what I did; I feel confident of that. By the way, I have received a very pressing invitation from Mrs. M—— to come, and bring my family with me, at an early opportunity, and, if you say so, we will go there some time soon; we will then see what you think of the South. I know you will change your opinion."

" I am not afraid of changing my opinion."

" Well, will you consent to go ?"

" I do not care much about mixing up with all those slave-holders. I feel that the very atmosphere would poison me."

" Do not talk that way ; what would Mrs. M—— think if she were to hear you talking so, after treating me with so much kindness ? I really blush to hear you speak thus. I wish I could prevail on you to make a visit South. I am anxious to enjoy that hospitality once more."

"Since you are so anxious to go, perhaps I will consent, just to see how things go on. I know I shall be glad to get back to my own home, again. I cannot countenance slavery anyhow; I think it a sin to own them, and it will have to be accounted for some day. I have often thought of the manner in which they live; do tell me about it."

"I did not stay there long enough to know much about that."

"I suppose you would have been disgusted if you had."

"Oh no, quite to the contrary. Mrs. M—— insisted upon my staying a few days, but I could not possibly do so. She said that she would like me to see for myself; she knew how much prejudice the Northerners have for those South. We are under a wrong impression."

"A wrong impression, indeed! I know that all the people South could not get me to alter my opinion."

"I would not like to trust you. But you asked me to tell you something about the manner in which the slaves live at the South. Each family has a neat little cabin, nicely furnished, to which is attached a garden, and they work in it for themselves, and raise their own poultry. They have certain holidays, and on these occasions they enjoy themselves by dancing, or in any manner they please. It would really do you good to see how they enjoy themselves. On Saturday nights, after having completed their week's labor, they go to their cabins and regale themselves. I have never seen half the happiness North, among the servants, that I saw South. You can see for yourself, when you go.

It is not my design to endeavor to impress you with ideas about the South, only so far as what I know to be the truth, and nothing but the truth."

"Who was the gentleman with whom you stayed?"

"A Mr. M——, a very wealthy planter. He has two lovely and interesting children; they were so very polite and kind to the slaves. There is quite an aged woman there, whom they call Phebe; she used to be the nurse of his little daughter, and she loves her very much. I heard her tell her mother, the evening I was there, that she was going into Aunt Phebe's cabin to read to her. There was a delicate looking little slave there whom they called Hannah; she was a playmate of Mrs. M——'s little girl, of whom she was very fond. I do not think she will live long. Mrs. M—— seemed to be very anxious about her health when I was there, and she was under the charge of a physician then."

"Why, I thought that, no matter how sick the slaves were, their owners did not pretend to send for any doctor!"

"You see that is just what I tell you. Now I know this to be true about the little slave, for she was regularly attended by the physician."

"Perhaps it was all a sham."

"How very incredulous you are. Why should she try to deceive me? I do not know what benefit she could derive from it."

"Why, give the Southerners a good name."

"No, she has no such motives; and, besides, the physician told me himself, the evening I spent there, that she had been under his charge for six months, and that she received as much attention from her mistress as though she were white. This came from his own lips; I know it to be a truth, certainly."

"Well, I hope that slavery at the South is not so bad as it has been represented to be, yet I cannot help thinking it wrong," said Mrs. I——. "I suppose it is at the South as it is everywhere else, there are both good and bad people; some, I imagine, are kinder to their slaves than others."

"Well, that may be true, I admit; yet I really think that you will not find that cruelty in any one place at the South, which persons here are so inclined to believe is practised there."

"I think you are mistaken, Mr. I——, for many are cruelly treated there."

"I see it is of no use to try to convince you how erroneous the idea is. Besides, what right have you to believe that they are badly treated? Have you ever had a demonstration of it?"

"No, but I have had it from good authorities."

"Good authorities, indeed! I suppose some of our own people have written upon the subject, and you have read a pack of exaggerations, which are usually the contents of such works."

"I declare you have turned Southerner. What a tact they have for proselyting people."

"They have not proselyted me, by any means; but they have convinced me that I had an entirely wrong opinion of slavery."

"Then you believe in slave-holding?"

"I did not say that I was any advocate for slavery, but I say this much, that so long as they are treated well, and have kind owners, let them remain as such.

I will never be the one to try to entice them away from their owners. I do not believe that a trusty, grateful slave would leave his master anyhow, for he knows well enough that he is kindly treated, and when he has. a good home he had better keep it."

" One objection I have to slavery is, the ignorance in which they are kept at the South. Why are they not taught to read and write as well as ourselves ?"

" They are taught ; for I heard Mrs. M——, myself, call in two. of the younger slaves to instruct them, and I stood by and heard them say the alphabet. Now say that is a sham."

" I suppose the alphabet was all they knew."

" Well, what if it was ? they are very young, and must learn the alphabet before they can learn anything. Which did you learn first, to read, or the A, B, C ?"

" Poor creatures ! I don't suppose they will ever get any farther than .the alphabet !"

" Never mind, time will show; just wait until we make our visit South, and we will see how much they know ; for your especial benefit, I will have them called in and examined. I wonder how many of our white servants this very moment don't know A from B ?"

" It is because they have no one to teach them ; it is true that we have a plenty of free-schools, but they have no time to go, and by that means they are kept in ignorance."

" There is just where a slave has the advantage ; he has a kind master to instruct him after his daily work is done, and finds great pleasure in teaching him. But the poor white servants have not a moment's time to learn anything. Now, who of the Northerners would willingly pay them as though they worked, and let them have that time to go to free-schools ?"

"The slaves South get no pay at all; they work all the time, and then never get a shilling."

"I think they get a fair remuneration; indeed, I am sure they are allowed some time to work for themselves. They are well fed and clothed; if they are sick, every attention is paid them; they are sheltered from the cold; protected from the scorching sun. Now, what more can they expect? Look at some of our poor laborers, who have to work in all kinds of weather, both hot and cold; see how unprotected they are. Look at some of our white slaves who get sick, and die from the want of proper attention being paid them, and in case the physician is called in, they have the bill to pay themselves. I wish you to consider all this; I never weighed the matter fairly until I went South, and saw how differently the slaves were treated from what they have been represented to be."

"But do you not think that the very consciousness our servants have of their freedom, renders them contented ?"

"Pray what good does their freedom do them, when they very often suffer for the comforts of life? They have to toil as hard as a Southern slave, and even harder. Oh! it is merely a name—'freedom'—for they are not any happier in the possession of it than if they had owners. I find it no use to argue with you."

"I see very plainly that your head has been turned

by those Southerners, and, for my part, I heartily wish you had never seen them."

"So much for a good example being set. If I had not thought they acted in a just manner, I never would have believed what I do. I think it would be of great service to you and some of our other Northern people to go South, and see how they treat their slaves; perhaps it would teach them how to act towards their white slaves. Depend upon it, it would do your heart good to spend a month at the South, and partake of their hospitality. I'll venture that you would never want to come North again, not even on a visit."

"I will see for myself, when I go there. I am not at all uneasy about getting so much attached to it. I am thinking that I would be so much disgusted that I would be for coming right home again."

"We people North do not understand living," said Mr. I——. "We know nothing of those comforts which are to be found there; there is all the difference in the world between the North and South. If you want to see hospitality or warm-heartedness, just go South. Why, you feel just as perfectly at home with them in a few days, as you do in a month, North. I'll venture to say that you'll not be likely to live next door to any one in the South for a month, and even a year, without their calling upon you. Why, some people here don't even know your name, although you lived next to them a whole year."

"Well, you know we are more reserved."

"I will admit that we are more cold-hearted. I must go to my office now, for I promised to write to

Mr. M—— on my arrival home, and must fulfil my promise.''

So off goes Mr. I—— to his office, to write, while his wife reflects upon the conversation, and is very much afraid that he will turn Southerner in his notions, in spite of all her remonstrances.

CHAPTER VIII.

MADORA AT SCHOOL.

Two months have passed away since Madora left home. She now began to feel much more at home, and began to get very much attached to the girls. She had been a great pet at home, yet she knew that the rules of the school must be obeyed, and felt that the best way to gain the love and esteem of the teachers was to conform to them.

Madora was a universal favorite; her amiability and gentleness of disposition won the love of all the girls. Even the older ones loved her society, and she was considered among them as a great pet.

She had received several letters from her mother, and was very punctual in the answering of them.

Mrs. M—— noticed with delight the progress her daughter was making, and saw what a marked difference there was between the first letters of Dora and the last ones which she had written. There was less childishness about them, and that was one great obstacle removed. Mrs. M—— often wished that she was not so child-like, but she hoped that, by sending her away from home for awhile, where she would not get so much petting, it would be of great service to her.

Mrs. P—— kept her advised of the progress which

Dora made, as she had promised, and it was with no small delight that she read the words of commendation which were contained in the letters. Mrs. P—— stated in her letter that there was a particular point in Dora's character which she so much admired, and that was her innocency. Then she noticed how strictly she regarded the rules of the school, and the attention she paid to her studies.

Mrs. M—— wrote very frequently to Dora, and spoke to her of the importance of conducting herself in a becoming manner, and it afforded her much gratification to find that her advice was heeded. Although Dora had never been in the habit of disobeying her, yet she feared lest, among so many, she might possibly be influenced.

Those who have been educated at boarding-schools know full well the diversity of character and disposition there found. Some have less art about them than others; some are more attentive to rules than others. Such, indeed, was the case at the institute of Mrs. P——.

She was extremely attentive to the deportment of her scholars, and often spoke to them of the importance of acting in such a way as not to merit any reproach whatever. She had taken a great interest in Dora, seeing her innocency, and knowing, too, that she had been the object of such anxiety to her parents. Often she would send for her, and talk to her very kindly, and in such a manner as caused a great love to spring up in the youthful heart of Dora.

Two months at boarding-school is quite a period, so

9

far as events are concerned; for many things transpire in that space of time, short as it may seem.

Dora had become, as we have said before, much attached to her school-mates, and particularly to Lydia B——. They were almost always together, and ever shared each other's troubles. Dora had often written to her mother about Lydia, and expressed a strong attachment for her. She had fully determined the first time she went home, that she should accompany her. Lydia partially consented to the kind invitation of her friend, and said, with the permission of her parents, she would go. It would, however, be quite a long time, yet she had a delightful visit in the prospective.

Dora's vacation was to be spent in travelling about to different places, as she was such a distance from home it would not be convenient for her to return every vacation.

Lydia did not live far from the institution, consequently she always spent her vacations at home, and made Dora promise to go with her some time. It was agreed upon that she should spend her second vacation there, for she could not prevail on Dora to accompany her the first, as she was anticipating a visit to the Falls. She had never been there, yet her vivid imagination pictured the lovely scenes to her; even then she heard the roaring of the Falls, and saw the water gliding like a sheet of silver over the rocks.

"Oh, how delighted I shall be," said she, "to visit the Falls. I only wish, dear Lydia, that you could go with us; I know you would be charmed."

"I was there last summer."

"Were you, indeed? How were you pleased?"

"I could not possibly tell you how charmed I was. Oh! it is so sublime, Dora; I know you will wish to visit there again. But you must not get so infatuated with your trip that you will prefer making a visit there again next summer to going home with me."

"You need not fear anything of that sort. I will certainly go with you, for mamma says I can; she told me so in the last letter I got from her. I will be sure not to disappoint you. I was thinking, the other day, what I should do when you leave school; you know you leave a year before myself."

"Do not think so far ahead, dear Dora. You know we will have at least five years to stay together; do not begin to think of the parting yet. I always look upon the bright side of the picture; and you find that persons who do that are always happier."

"I will not think of our parting any more, then, until the time comes. I expect that five years will glide away very rapidly to me; for, in spite of myself, I will often find that I am reflecting on our parting."

Month after month quickly fled, and now examination time was drawing near. All of the girls were preparing for it. Now they were deeply engaged with their studies. An examination was something very novel for Dora; she scarcely knew what it was; it was not, as it might be expected, a very pleasant subject to reflect upon, by any means.

"Do tell me," said she one day, to Lydia, "what do you have to go through at the examination? Are you not always very much frightened?"

" Yes, indeed! But all we have to do is to prepare for it. For my part, I am always glad when the time comes for examination, for then, after that, we always go home. But I do not think I will be much delighted this time, because I will have to part with you."

" Now I thought I told you never to mention the subject of our parting again, and now you are talking about the very same thing."

" Oh, I forgot; I will not do so any more."

To a school-girl, an examination is always much dreaded; although she may be prepared in her studies, yet she fears lest she might fail, for it requires quite a good deal of courage sometimes. The idea of being in the presence of so many persons as are generally present at a public examination, is very embarrassing indeed, especially to those who have never been subjected to one.

Dora was diligent in the preparation of her studies, for she expected her parents and brother on the occasion, and she also wished to do credit to herself and her instructors. Filled, too, with the idea of the delightful trip she anticipated at its close, it seemed to impel her onward. Her letters were less frequent home, in consequence of being so much occupied with her studies; but her mother knew the cause, consequently felt no uneasiness whatever..

Aunt Phebe continued to inquire very anxiously each day after Dora, and wondered why her young "missus didn't send a letter home, now-a-days." In spite of all Mrs. P——'s explanations, she declared that " de Norrud folks would make dat chil' study too hard, anyhow, and she didn't 'spect to see no roses on her cheeks no-how, 'caze she larnt too much in de big books."

Mrs. M—— wrote to Dora, and told her what Aunt Phebe said, and she laughed heartily at the idea, and sent Aunt Phebe word not to be uneasy about her; that she would not study too hard, and said she would take good care of herself.

Mrs. M—— read the message Dora sent Aunt Phebe. The good old soul cried; she said that "Miss Dora was a blessed good chil', and she b'lieved dat she was an angel, anyhow." She was extremely anxious to see Dora, but knew that it would be a very long time yet.

" Missus, when do you 'spect to see Miss Dora ?"

" Very soon, Aunt Phebe, perhaps in about a month from now."

" Is she gwine to come home ?"

" No, but I am going to see her, and take her tra-velling."

" Vel, I wish Phebe could go, an' if it wa'n't for de ole man, I would go; for I knowed you would let me go—wouldn't you, missus ?"

" Yes, Aunt Phebe; you know I need a servant to travel with me. Could you not leave Uncle Dick ?"

" Why, bless my soul, no, missus; couldn't leab de ole man, nohow; he's too poorly, and if Phebe goes away and leabs him, den he tinks I don't care nuffin' 'bout him. Well, missus, yer ken tell her how much I wants to see her, and gib a mighty heap ob love to her; bless her sweet soul, I wishes I could see her now."

" You are very much attached to Dora, and I know she thinks a great deal of you, for she always mentions you in her letters."

9*

"Yes, marm, missus, dat she does; Phebe knowed dat."

"To-morrow is examination," exclaimed Lydia. "Dear me, I do dread it so much. I have studied my lessons, yet I know that among so many persons I shall get frightened."

"Mamma will be here too, to-morrow," said Dora. "Just think what a long time it has been since I have seen her; how happy will be the meeting. Brother Charles, of whom you have so often heard me speak, is coming too. He will go with papa, who came on for the purpose of selecting some college for him to go to."

"Then will he return home with him?"

"No, he will not go home again for some time; perhaps not until I go. Oh! how I wish examination was over, for I do dread it; but I hope it will not be so bad as I think."

"I hope not; I expect we will all come off better than we expect to, I hope so, at least. I know how frightened I was the first time, and I laughed at myself afterwards for my folly. There, the study-bell is ringing, and I must leave you. Good-night."

To-morrow came; the much dreaded examination was about to take place. There were, as expected, many spectators, and now all the girls repair to the schoolroom. How anxious do they all appear now; they look at each other meaningly, as much as to say, "I wonder if I will miss?"

Dora was looking out very anxiously for her parents, and every bell she heard made her heart palpitate.

As it happened, Dora's seat was near an open window; she was not engaged in any class at that hour. On looking out, who should she see but her parents coming. She could scarcely refrain from giving vent to her joy. She asked permission of one of the teachers to leave the room; suspecting her motive for so doing, she allowed her to go.

She had scarcely got to the door, before she was in her mother's arms. "Dora"—"mamma," was all they could say. One who has been absent for a long time from home, can imagine how delightful it is to meet their parents and friends.

As Dora was to be examined in the next class, she hastened with her parents up to the school-room, and took her accustomed seat.

Lydia, who was sitting opposite, saw her when she entered with her parents. She was equally as much delighted as Dora; seeing her so happy caused a responsive feeling in her own heart. She was in anticipation, too, of her own parents.

Class after class was examined, until it was time for the examination to close for the day. Of this, Dora was heartily glad, for she had not seen her parents for so long, that it was really a treat to be with them once more.

"Where is your friend Lydia," asked Mrs. M——, of Dora?"

"I really forgot to bring her; but I was so much engaged with my own thoughts, and so delighted to see you, that I forgot to bring her."

In a minute away skipped Dora to find her friend.

"Well, Lydia, here you are, just as I expected—

studying away for life. Come with me; mamma is anxious to see you."

In a few minutes Dora came, hand in hand, with Lydia. Mrs. M—— was quite delighted with her, and expressed a wish that she would accompany them to the Falls. But this kind offer Lydia declined, by saying that she was anxious to spend the summer home, and besides, she went to the Falls last summer.

"You must be sure, Mrs. M——, to let Dora go home with me, next summer."

"Yes, my dear; if nothing happens to prevent, I will let her go with you."

The examination lasted a week. There is little variation, anyhow, in them, so that it was pretty much the same thing, except the last day, which was confined to music and composition-reading.

After its close, Dora and her parents left for their trip. But now, a trial was to come; Dora was compelled to part with Lydia, and although she knew it would be but a brief time, yet she felt very sad about leaving her, for a day even.

After much affectionate interchange of sentiment, and a fond embrace, they parted with the hope of soon meeting again.

Dora, with her parents, full of joyful spirits, now commenced her long expected and much desired trip to Niagara. She had heard and read so much about it, that she had a great curiosity to see the place. Her parents could not have delighted her more than by giving her a trip to that sublime and magnificent spot, which ever fills the mind of all those who behold it with awe and admiration.

CHAPTER IX.

MADORA AT NIAGARA.

"WHAT is that roaring noise I hear, papa? It must be the Falls. I had no idea that we were so near."

"We are much farther from them, my dear, than you think we are; the roaring is heard at a very great distance off."

"Oh! I wish I were there now, for I am so anxious to see them. How much I would like Lydia to be with us."

"It would have been a great deal of company for you, my dear, and nothing would have afforded me greater pleasure than having her with us."

In about two hours after the conversation commenced, they were in sight of the Falls.

It is impossible to describe the delight of Dora. She thought she had never seen anything so grand before.

"Only look, papa! how clear the water is, and how it glides over the rocks. Oh! I feel as though I would never tire of this place."

"It is the novelty, my dear, which pleases you so much. I dare say you would tire of it, as is generally the case when novelty ceases. You might ever admire it, for one could not look upon this sublime piece of work without being filled with admiration. It will afford you a theme for composition, when you return to school, and I shall expect you to write upon it, and send me a copy."

"But, papa, what could my feeble language do in the way of description? I am sure I would fail in the attempt."

"I do not expect a masterpiece from you, by any means, because you are very young, yet; but you can do your best, and that will answer for me."

One morning, while Dora was much engaged, enjoying the Falls, the thought occurred to her that it was her birthday. Her father, seeing her in a very thoughtful mood, asked of what she was thinking.

"Do you know, papa, that this is my birthday? I am now thirteen years old. Just think! I am in my teens!"

"So it is your birthday? Dear me, how time passes away. It seems but yesterday that you were a little wee child, sitting on my knee; but now you are almost a young lady in size."

"But not in age, papa."

"Oh! no, not yet. You really have grown very rapidly since you left home; I think you will be quite tall when you have attained your full size. If you don't mind, your age will get the better of you."

"I promised to write Lydia a letter, and as this is my birthday, I think I will write to her this morning, after I get seated quietly in my room. If I defer it too long, she will think I am inconstant, or that I have forgotten her, and I am not very ambitious to have her think either. She has, indeed, been a true friend to me, and I do not know what I should do without her. We were talking about that the other day, when we would no longer be school-mates; she leaves at least a year before I do. Never mind, I have one consolation, we will be there a long time together before we do part."

The sun was getting rather warm, so Dora and her father returned to the hotel, where she found her mother waiting for them.

"Did it occur to you, mamma, that this is my birthday?"

"Really, my dear, I had forgotten it."

"I am in my teens, mamma; just think of it!"

"Yes, my dear, life passes rapidly away with us; yet we do not notice how it glides from us; each hour, each minute, brings life nearer to a close. Twelve months have indeed flown; how many changes, too, have taken place in that length of time."

"I thought, mamma, that, as it was my birthday, I would write to Lydia; you know I promised to do so when we parted. I told her that so soon as I arrived here, and had taken a good view of the Falls, I would write. She said she expected that when I got here I would forget her, and if I do not hurry and write, she will think that I have forgotten her, sure enough."

Dora hastened to her chamber, and sat near an open window, it being a very delightful day, and commenced her letter to Lydia.

"MY CHERISHED FRIEND :—

"It is a lovely, lovely morn. The sun shines brightly, and now I am seated by my window, which is beautifully shaded with trees, enjoying the delightful breeze, which so softly whispers through the green foliage. The little birds are on light wing, gayly singing, and, as they pass my window, how I wish they would fly to you, and bear my love to your own sweet self. Niagara! Oh, Eden spot, what shall I say of it? 'Tis beautiful, passing beautiful. As I look around, and enjoy all these beauties, I feel there is but one thing wanting, and that is the presence of my own dear Lydia.

"This is my birthday, dear friend. Yes, twelve months have passed away, and again comes this important day. As I look back upon the past, how many recollections arise in my mind. I think of my sweet southern home, where many happy days have been spent; I remember the sweet magnolia vale, where oft, at sunset's hour, I've wandered, and inhaled the rich perfume which the zephyr bore upon its wing from that queenlike flower. Methinks I see it now, enshrouded in its snowy robe, as if some angel had strayed there, and left its garment upon the green leaves, and the magnolia, admiring its beauty, claimed it for her own.

"I hear the voice of streams, and the gentle rustling of leaves. Ah, yes! fond memory wanders to those scenes, and I sigh to think that twelve months more of my life have passed away. But so it must be, for time waits not for us, but is ever winging its flight away.

"The season here is very gay; the place is crowded with visitors, and I have met with several of my own age. We all pass our time very pleasantly indeed. Yet do not for a moment think that I am forgetting you; I think of you each day, and love you the same as ever. No, dearest, do not let your little heart allow jealousy to enter it, for I assure you there is not the least cause for it. I will write you again soon; until then, adieu. Think, sometimes, of your absent but attached

"DORA."

Having finished the letter, Dora read it over, then sent it immediately, for she felt that she had delayed writing too long already.

"Well, mamma, I have come now to have a nice chat with you. I have finished my letter to Lydia, sealed, and sent it. I am glad that it is gone, and shall feel quite uneasy until it is received. I would not have her think that I cease to care for her, for anything in the world."

"Do not be uneasy, my child. She knows very well that your long silence has not been without some very good cause. She knows how it is here; for she thinks, I dare say, of last summer, when she was here herself."

"We have only three more weeks to stay here, mamma."

"Yes, that is all, my dear; you know we must go to Saratoga and several other places, before our trip is out. I am anxious to have you see all you can, and hope you will profit by your tour. When you return to school you will have recreated, and be ready again for your studies, which I hope you will pursue with as much ardor as before."

"I shall really be glad to get there again for one thing, and that is to see Lydia. I expect she is equally as anxious to see me. What a happy meeting it will be, and how much we shall have to tell each other. It will be two months since we have seen each other, and a great many things can transpire in that length of time."

"Yes, my dear, two months make a great difference in many things; many sorrows and many joys have been shared in that length of time."

The morning previous to Dora and her mother leaving for the Falls, some one rapped at the door.

Dora opened it, and a waiter handed her a letter.

How hastily did she break the seal, for the well-known handwriting of Lydia was seen on the back.

10

"Oh! mamma, mamma, I have a letter from Lydia; I cannot read it fast enough."

"Do not be impatient, my dear," said her mother.

Lydia's letter was full of deep feeling and pure affection, which emanated from her heart. She spoke of the time when they should meet again, and seemed impatient for it to arrive.

"In a few weeks," wrote Lydia, "we, dear Dora, shall meet again. Oh! would that it were to-morrow; that I could behold your sweet face again, and the smile which ever gladdens my heart. It seems an age since I saw you, and it has been but a short time since we parted. All I ask of you, my dear friend, is, that you will not forget Lydia; she who ever dreams of you at evening's hour, and who ever keeps your image before her eyes. I have a thousand things to tell you, but will wait until we meet. Adieu, my loving friend, and still love your attached Lydia."

Dora's eyes were suffused with tears as she read this letter; she knew it came from the heart; for Lydia was indeed a being of fidelity, and affection breathed in every word of her letter to Dora.

Some have said that school-girls' friendship is not lasting; this is a mistaken idea, indeed; for many friendships formed at school continue through life, which may be clearly shown in the case of Lydia and her friend.

Three weeks soon passed away; they would seem brief indeed at such a place as Niagara, where there is so much to interest the mind. Besides the magnificent and grand scenery, there are thousands of strangers coming every day, and it is pastime even to observe the different manners and customs of the persons around us. Dora, as we have said, was very observing, consequently she had enough to employ her mind; being very winning, too, in her manners, she attracted the notice of many. Persons judging from her size and manners in general would have taken her to be much older than she was in reality. A year had made a great difference, indeed, in her. She had improved very rapidly while at the seminary of Mrs. P——, in consequence of her attention to her studies; and being away from home, she would now have to think for herself. It happened one day, as she was rambling about, she missed her way. She was not far from the hotel. She had gone out a little while to enjoy a walk alone, and reflect upon the theme on which her father had desired her to write. Finding that she had missed her way she became a little alarmed, although she knew that she had not wandered far.

Much to her delight, she saw some one coming; her fears now entirely abated, for she knew that she had seen the same person at the hotel. He was a youth, apparently not more than seventeen years of age, very handsome, and his complexion showed him to be a Northerner. What to do, Dora could not divine; she did not like to speak to him; but, at last, she found that she was compelled to make a virtue of necessity; so, without any farther hesitancy, she told him that she had lost her way, and would be obliged if he would show her the way to the hotel. He had seen Dora several times at the hotel, and thought her particularly handsome. He had inquired her name, and was truly delighted to find an opportunity of rendering her any service.

It seems that the gentleman whom she met had gone to the Falls for the purpose of recreating a little; his health had been precarious, but had improved very rapidly, as might be seen from his brilliant complexion.

Dora, much to her surprise, learned that his name was Mr. B——. "I wonder," thought she, "if he is Lydia's brother? It cannot be, for she would have told me that her brother would be here.

It happened, though, that he had gone there rather unexpectedly, and Lydia did not know anything of it. When he left college, he was not determined as to what place he would go; and, besides, when he last wrote, he was at Saratoga, and thought he should go from thence to the Virginia Springs.

Dora was indeed delighted to find that it was Lydia's brother; and, as he was going directly home from there, she had a fine opportunity of sending verbal messages.

"I have met with quite an adventure, mamma, this morning."

"What was it, my dear?"

"Well, I went out to take a little ramble, and I lost my way."

"Just like you, Miss Romance; well, what else?"

"I did not know what I should do; so I just waited very patiently, and, in a few minutes, I saw some one coming towards me. It was a young gentleman, and I was compelled to ask him to show me the way, although it was very embarrassing for me to speak to a stranger. Who do you think it was?"

"I cannot imagine, really!"

"Lydia B——'s brother!"

" The brother of the young lady with whom you were so intimate at boarding-school?"

" The very same."

" Well, I declare; you have met with a pleasing adventure, indeed."

" He leaves to-morrow morning early; I shall have a fine chance to send lots of messages."

" Did you have an introduction, or just merely scrape acquaintance as you came along."

" Why, I met my friend Fanny L——, and she introduced us after we had gone but a few steps, as I gave her to understand that I did not know his name. I assure you it served to relieve me a great deal, for I was very much embarrassed. It is near time for me to write the letter I intend sending by him, and I think I had better retire. I will scarcely know where to stop, for I have so much to say. How unexpected was the adventure with which I met!"

" You had better hurry, Dora, for darkness will overtake you; and I suppose you cannot resume the letter after tea, for I know you have made some engagement."

" You are right, mamma; I promised Mr. B—— to play for him upon the guitar. He proposes making up a little party, consisting of Fanny, Mr. L——, and you, mamma, to go out and take a moonlight ramble, and then find some pleasant spot to seat ourselves, and I will play for you all. Will you go, mamma?"

" O yes, my dear."

" Very well; remember your promise," said Dora, as she skipped along; in a few minutes she was conversing on paper with her friend Lydia.

CHAPTER X.

AUNT PHEBE—MR. AND MRS. M—— RETURN HOME.

When Mrs. M—— left home, she gave directions to Aunt Phebe to have everything in nice order when she should return; consequently, she set about giving the house a thorough cleansing from top to bottom. The thoughts of the pleasure it would give her mistress to come home and find everything in such nice order, and the commendation which she would receive, spurred her on. Aunt Phebe was remarkable for her neatness, and whenever she set about doing anything she always did it in the best manner.

"I do wonder when missus is gwine to come home. For my part, I really is tired waitin' for her; I wants to hear from dat ar' chil', an' I knows dat she sont me some word."

Uncle Dick, who was busy whitewashing, was making all possible haste; "'caze he didn't want missus," as he said, "to come home and cotch dat ar' stuff all ober de floor." He was putting the last coat of wash on, much to his delight. Aunt Nelly and Laura were washing the paints in the rooms up stairs, which Uncle Dick had finished two days before.

Aunt Phebe made it her business, every now and then, to come up, to see that they were doing it well; at the same time telling them that "dey had better hurry, 'caze dey didn't know when missus might come home."

However, they got through their cleaning in a little while, much to the gratification of Aunt Phebe. The next thing to set about was her cabin. She was careful to get all the cooking apparatus finished first, and then her own cabin. Moses and Cary had to be very particular now about their feet; for Aunt Phebe was dreadfully afraid they would soil the highly-polished floor before her mistress could get a peep at it.

Uncle Dick, who had the faculty (as all the slaves on the plantation said) of seeing things before they came, was sitting at the cabin door. At last he says: " Ole ooman, somehow I tinks dat missus will be here to-day. Yer will see if it ain't so; yer knows I kin tell tings anyhow afore dey come."

" Well, I hopes dey will; 'caze I wants to see 'em."

" Dar dey come ! dar dey come !" said Uncle Dick. " Didn't I tell yer so ? I knowed it."

Upon that, Aunt Phebe went out, and in a few minutes saw her mistress.

" Well, missus, I'se mighty glad to see you. I'se been waitin' for yer dis long time. I'se been habbin' de house cleaned up for yer, and I told dem dar niggers dat you would come afore dey knowed it."

" I see, Phebe, that you have attended strictly to my directions about the house. I knew when I told you that when I came home I should find things just as I would wish. I have brought you all presents. You know that I take great pleasure in rewarding you all, and you will not go unpaid for your labor, and the pains which you exert in my behalf."

"De Lors bless yer, missus, if you ain't too good. I knowed you would remember Phebe; I said dat fust. But, missus, I didn't do de work 'caze I wanted yer to pay me; I did it 'caze I lubed yer, and liked to please yer."

"I know all that very well, Phebe, and appreciate your motives; but you know I always like to show that I remember my slaves when I am away from them."

"Missus, I wants yer to tell me 'bout dat chil'; how do she look?"

"I never saw her look better in all my life, Phebe. She is as gay as a bird."

"I'se mighty feared dat she will kill herself, larnin' in dem great books."

"O no, Phebe; she takes good care that she doesn't injure her health. When you see her you will not know her, she has grown so much."

"I don't 'spect I will, sure 'nuff."

"I really believe she has caught a beau, Aunt Phebe."

"Cotch a beau! I tought so! I said, when dey told me yer was gwine to dat great place, dat she would break all de hearts of de gemmen."

"He is a Northerner."

"A Norruder! Why, de Lors bless my soul. I don't wants her to hab dem, nohow; 'caze den she will git a 'litionist, right off."

"O no, Phebe; she will always have her Southern principles."

"Well, I knows one ting; she midn't be afeared to trus' Phebe wid her, 'caze I ain't nebber gwine to let dem 'litionists 'suade me off, nohow. I rudder be her slave, any time."

Uncle Dick's first question was, "How's Massa Charlie?"

"He was very well, Uncle Dick, when I left him at college."

"O yes, missus, I 'members now; you know dat I can't recollect tings like I used ter. I'se mighty sorry he has gone 'way, but den I can't help it. I hopes I will see him 'gin. Didn't he tell yer to tell me nuffin?"

"Yes, he sent you his love; and says you must take good care of his kite, against he comes home."

"Dat I will, missus. I'se got it put away now, an' I bound no one don't tar' it, nohow; but I don't 'spects dat he will fly it any more, 'caze when he comes home he will be too big. De Lors bless poor ole Uncle Dick; he ain't got nobody to lub him now. Nebber mind, young master lub him. Missus, when I gwine to see him 'gin? Nebber, I'se feared."

"O yes, you will, Uncle Dick; he will come home some time. He won't forget you."

"Vel, I hopes not, missus."

In a few minutes all the slaves had come to the house to welcome their owners home. They were truly glad to see them, for they were much attached to Mr. and Mrs. M——. They always acted in such a manner towards them, they could but love and respect them.

"Well, massa," said Rufus, "I'se mighty glad dat you has come; my boots is waring out."

"Didn't I tell yer so," said Aunt Phebe; "I knowed dat you would dance 'em all out, afore massa come home."

"Which are you glad to see, Rufus," said Mr. M—— (much amused at the salutation he had given him), your master, or the means to get the boots?"

"Why, massa, I be glad to see yer; I only just mentioned dat, to let yer know dat dey was waring out."

"Oh, I understand you very well, Rufus; I will get you a pair of boots very soon. I suppose you have been behaving yourself since I have been gone; hasn't he, Aunt Phebe?"

"Well, yes, sar, massa; de only ting dat I habs 'gainst him is, dat he will dance all de starch out. de collars, arter I stiffen 'em."

"If that is the only fault, I am very well satisfied. You all can come in after dinner, and I will see what presents I have brought you."

After Rufus got outside the door, he could scarcely contain himself; he and Laura went dancing around, at a great rate, quite elated with the thoughts of the presents they were going to get.

"I do wonder," said Aunt Phebe, "what makes dat ar' nigger sich a fool? If massa habs got somefing for him, he jist as well 'have himself as not; yer don't ketch dis nigger jumping round, nohow, 'caze I don't b'lieve in any sich actions."

Aunt Phebe was more hurried about dinner that day than she ever had been in her life. Uncle Dick said, more than once, that he wished ole ooman would hurry and sont de dinner in de house.

Rufus had put his nice white apron on earlier than usual, and was at Aunt Phebe's cabin door long before she was ready for him. Laura, too, had given her a call, and asked if dinner wasn't most ready.

Aunt Phebe by this time had become quite irritated, and said that "if dem ar' niggers didn't let her 'lone, she would sarve 'em a nice trick, by not getting dinner ready for two hours yet."

This menace had the desired effect, for they did not trouble her any more.

Rufus was particularly hasty in clearing away the table that day. Mr. and Mrs. M—— had not more than dined, before he went to work, and, much to the amusement of Mrs. M——, called in Laura to assist him. She did not feel much disposed to assist him, for she was anxious to eat her dinner, so as to be the first one to get her present. She knew, however, that it would never do to be disobliging to Rufus, so she obeyed his summons.

We will just stand behind the door, and see what effect the presents have upon the different slaves.

"Well, Rufus," said Mr. M——, "here are a nice pair of boots which I bought expressly for you."

"Yah! yah! yah!" echoed Rufus, "didn't I know dat? Look at 'em, any gemman might be proud on 'em; but wont dis nigger dance now?"

"I 'specks yer will dance 'em all out afore yer knows it, like yer did the tothers," said Aunt Phebe.

Rufus, after having received his present, remained to see what fell to the lot of the others.

"Ben, here is a banjo for you!"

"Egad! an dat ar' an' de boots will go togedder. Tank yer sar, massa, yer could'nt please me better, it sounds beautiful," said Ben, as he touched the chords; "an' wont dis nigger 'sprise dese niggers heels? I will dat. We must hab a dance soon."

" Dick, I purchased you a nice large cane; I know
that you are getting old now, and I often see you with
a stick which you cut from the trees.. I brought you a
coat, too, for I know the one you have now is getting
quite shabby."

"Bless yer, massa, for tinking of poor ole Uncle
Dick; he nebber forgits yer in dis world. Tank yer,
tank yer, a thousand times, massa. Ole Dick has
sarved you dese many years, and he will sarve yer faithful still; he nebber leab yer till de good Being call him
home to glory, and den he must go."

" Phebe," said Mrs. M——, " I brought you a nice
head-handkerchief; see the colors, how bright they are."

" It's mighty purty, missus!"

" Here is a white apron Dora sent you; she made it
herself, and told me to give it to Aunt Phebe, and tell
her, whenever she wore it, to think of her."

" Bless dat child, I lubs her; I see she ain't gwine
to forgit me, nohow, toe."

Aunt Nelly now came forward to the call of Mrs.
M——. A black dress was given her, and at the same
time a neat pocket-handkerchief, hemmed by Dora's
own hand.

" Tank yer, missus; and when yer writes to Miss
Dora, tell her dat she is mighty good to ole Aunt
Nelly."

Laura was getting very impatient now, and was wishing that Aunt Nelly would stop "dat talking, hindering
missus from gibben her her present."

" Well, Laura, here is a dress for you. I heard you
say one day that you would like to have a dress of this

kind, so I got it for you. Here is a collar Dora sent you."

"Oh! ain't it purty? I'se much 'bliging, missus, to yer; when I said dat I wanted dat ar' dress, I didn't ting nothing 'bout yer gittin' it for me; yer is a mighty good missus."

The other slaves of the plantation each received something from their owners, who never liked to show any partiality whatever to them, lest it should raise a feeling of discontent. They were all very much delighted with their presents, as it proved to them that they were not forgotten.

"I declare," said Aunt Phebe, after she went into her cabin; "we ought to be mighty tankful dat we is so well off as we is. I knows dat my missus is de best creature in de world."

"Does yer see dis ar' cane?" said Uncle Dick, "ain't it illegant? Won't I walk, too; and look at dis ar' coat, ole ooman; yer must put it way and keep it mighty nice for me. Only jist listen to dat ar' foolish Ben busting open dat ar' new banjo what masser fotch him. I tole yer so, it is jist like him."

"Well, ole man, he wants to try it, ter see how it goes. I 'specks we will all git tired 'nuff of hearing it play."

"Young folks will be young folks," said Uncle Dick.

"Dey ain't 'blige to be so foolish, doe. Dars Rufus, now, I 'specks he wants me ter put some starch somewhar for him."

"Aunt Phebe, I say, has yer got my standin' collar done?"

"Is dat de way to ax for it? I'll knock yer down!"

Rufus did not reply to her in an impertinent manner,

11

for he was too anxious to get the collar; he thought he could possibly get around her by asking her pardon.

"I 'pologizes, Aunt Phebe, for speaking in sich a bruff manner; I did not mean anyting at all. Please, marm, will yer let me hab it to-morrow?"

Aunt Phebe became quite lenient at Rufus's apology, and told him that she would have it in readiness by to-morrow morning, being Sunday.

Away ran Rufus to Laura's cabin, to tell her that "he would make de plantation star' to-morrow, wid his new boots and standin' collar."

Rufus could not sleep much that night for thinking about his new boots; and he was up early enough the next morning; much elated at the idea of the figure he expected to make, and the excitement which he should create, among the negroes on the plantation.

CHAPTER XI.

LYDIA AND DORA—THE LETTER.

"At school again," said Dora, "and I am heartily glad of it. I was really quite tired of travelling, and am now glad to be quiet again. Yes, dear Lydia, you have been in my thoughts ever since I left you, and that is why I was so anxious to be back again. Two months have appeared brief to me, and how very many things transpire in that short time!"

"It is true, I feel a little homesick, Dora; but that is to be expected; for when one leaves her parents and friends she will be sad for a while. I think we shall both be very happy; and I am confident, that if meeting me affords you as much pleasure as it does me to meet you, we can but be contented."

"Indeed, I do not know what I should do without you, Lydia, for there seems to be a strong tie which binds me to this place; and I know very well that, if you were gone, there would be no longer a charm for me here."

This conversation occurred between the two friends shortly after their arrival at school.

At the commencement of a term at boarding-school, there is always quite a confusion. New classes have to be formed, new scholars are coming, and old ones returning after a vacation. As not much was doing,

Lydia and Dora had a fine opportunity of saying much to each other. Dora related the circumstance of meeting with Lydia's brother at the Falls, and Lydia, in return, expressed the pleasure it gave her, on the arrival of her brother, to find a letter from Dora.

" I was so much surprised," said Lydia ; "and Harry teazed me enough about it, before he would even let me see the direction ; but still, he told me it was from you, and, at first, I would not believe him."

" What did you think when you saw my handwriting?"

" Think ?   I did not know what to think.   I was all impatience until he explained it to me.   I thought it was a romantic piece of business, anyhow."

In a few days their studies were resumed, and they usually prepared their lessons together.   Every day the friendship between them seemed to grow stronger and stronger ; they were, in fact, almost inseparable.

" A letter ! a letter !" cried one of the girls.

" Who is it for?" asked three or four at once.

" It is directed to Lydia B——."

Lydia hearing this, rushed out in a moment, and saw the well-known handwriting of her brother.

" I see," said Lydia, after she had read it over, " he has not forgotten you ; see, he sends his best regards to you."

" I am certainly much obliged to him. I thought he had forgotten me long before this."

" You little rogue, you did not think any such thing. There goes the study-bell ; we shall have to wait for recitation, then we will go into the arbor and read it."

Dora was almost as anxious to read the letter as

Lydia, but she did not allow her curiosity to prevent her from studying. She soon got so much absorbed as to forget all about the letter, until the ringing of the bell announced recess.

"Come, Lydia," said Dora, "let us be off now, or else we shall not have time before the study-bell rings again."

After they had read the letter, Dora began to think how long it had been since she heard from home.

"I do really think, Lydia, that something must be the matter, for I know how very punctual mamma is in answering my letters. I do not expect papa to write often, for he has so much to attend to; and I always excuse him, for I know he will write whenever he can make it convenient. I know very well that something more than usual has occurred."

"O no; I hope not. You must not always be looking upon the dark side of the picture; that is one of your greatest failings."

"But I cannot help feeling badly about it, Lydia; and if I do not get a letter to-day, I shall give up in despair. I had a very strange dream last night about Aunt Nelly."

"Why, I hope you are not superstitious," said Lydia, laughing.

"O no, not at all; but I never dream of Aunt Nelly. It is the first time that I have dreamed of her since I left home. I really think that something will happen to her."

"Tell me your dream, Dora."

"Well, I cannot recollect it all. I know it was quite confused. I saw her all in robes of white; and then she had such a deathlike countenance. I thought she

11*

pointed to the grave right by little Hannah, and told me that she would lie there soon, and that I must come there sometimes. They were the last words that she told me when I left home; and one Sabbath evening, when I went with her to little Hannah's grave, she said that when I came back from school she would be lying there."

"You might have been thinking about her just before you went to sleep; persons often dream of what they reflect upon just before they retire."

"I never gave Aunt Nelly a thought before I went to sleep. I was thinking of nothing else but that lesson in history which we have to recite this afternoon. Oh! I do hope nothing will happen to Aunt Nelly, for I love her so much, and she has often told me that she loved me next to Hannah. She took me in her arms and cried bitterly when I bade her adieu. She said that something seemed to tell her that she should never see me again."

"Oh! you know what notions old people have sometimes, especially those slaves at the South; they believe in signs, and are extremely superstitious, anyhow. I hope you will not allow yourself to feel troubled, by any means, about your dream. I dare say that you will have one quite to the contrary to-night."

Lydia saw how distressed Dora seemed to feel, and thought of every way she could to pacify her. Lydia had thought it strange that she had had no tidings from home for quite a long time, yet she did not breathe her thoughts to Dora.

"Come, cheer up, Dora, do not look so sad; you will make me feel dreadfully if you do; and I know you would not willingly inflict a pain upon me, would you?"

"No, Lydia, for you know I love you too well for that; but I can't help feeling so. If I could just get a letter, I would rest perfectly content."

"Wait till the letters come; and, if you do not get one, it will be time enough then to feel impatient. Do not make trouble before it comes. There is the monitress now; I dare say she has a letter for you."

Sure enough, there was a letter for Dora; but it conveyed sad tidings to her. Her mother stated that the cause of her long silence was that Aunt Nelly had been very sick.

Mrs. M—— knew that it would cause Dora to feel very badly to hear such news, so she added that she need not feel any uneasiness whatever; that if Aunt Nelly got any worse, she would certainly advise her concerning it.

"There, I told you so," said Dora, weeping.

"Now, why do you grieve thus, my dear friend? Listen to what your mother tells you. Does she not say that you need not feel uneasy in the least, and that she will tell you if she gets any worse? Who knows, the next letter you get may bring the good news that she is so much better."

Dora's affection for Aunt Nelly is but one of the many instances of the love which the Southerners have for their slaves. Dora felt as much grieved, indeed, about Aunt Nelly, as though she had been a white person; and, after the reception of her mother's letter, containing an account of her illness, she could not study, for thinking about her.

Mrs. P——, noticing that she looked so dejected, sent for her, and thought that by talking to her she might possibly cheer up.

"What is the matter with you, Dora, my dear? It grieves me to see you looking, so sadly. That countenance does not become you. One like yourself should be all sunshine. You have every comfort which life affords—kind friends, idolizing·parents, a home of opulence. What more could you desire?"

Dora's tears started more freely.

"Why, child, why do you weep so?"

So soon as Dora could speak, she told Mrs. P—— that she had received a letter from her mother, the first one in a long time; and she told me that Aunt Nelly was very ill; and I am afraid I will never see her again. I know she talks about me, and would like to see me. If mamma would permit, I would start for home now, and see her."

"My dear, you must not give up to your feelings so. I do not expect she is as ill as you think. I dare say you will get another letter in a day. or two."

"Mamma promised she would write to me soon, and tell me about her."

"Why do you feel so badly? I sincerely hope that you will get a letter soon, saying she is much better."

"I am afraid she will be dead."

"Do not talk so. Do not expect such things. Always look at the bright side of an object. You are very young now, and if you give yourself up to looking for gloomy prospects, it will render you miserable. Life is now bright before you, my child; enjoy it while you can. Do not allow imaginary evils to trouble you.

When you get to be of my age, you will then laugh at your folly in allowing petty trials to grieve you. If you do not hear from your mother in a day or two, I will write myself. You can go now, my dear; and be sure to think of what I tell you. I am sorry to think you are so much grieved, and I know very well you have no cause for it at all."

Lydia had been waiting very impatiently for Dora, and was very glad when she saw her coming, wearing a more cheerful countenance. She was smiling through her tears. It looked like a gleam of sunshine through a cloud.

"Oh! I love Mrs. P——," said Dora; "she is so kind. You ought to have heard how sweetly she talked to me. She has the power to dispel the gloom of any one."

"Then she has chased away the cloud from round your heart?"

"Partially."

"Well, I am delighted to hear it, and sincerely hope that you will profit by her advice."

"You would feel as badly as I do, if you were placed in the same situation."

"I suppose I should, but would endeavor to govern my feelings."

"Oh! you do not know how good and kind dear old Aunt Nelly was to me. She used to love to hear me read to her, and would often come in my little chamber after she had kindled me a nice fire in the evening. She would get the Bible down, and ask me to read it for her. She is a dear, good old Christian. Pa offered her her freedom, but she would not accept it. She said she was happier as she was. You know she must have loved us all very much, to have wanted to stay. I felt more grief at parting with her than with any other slave on the plantation."

"Well, I suppose she thought she should never see you again ; but it is likely that she will see you as well as the rest. Come, do not get down into the suds again."

"I will try not, at least, for your sake, dear Lydia. I think I shall feel better to-morrow ; my head aches now."

"I thought that would be the case when you were crying so much. I hope that to-morrow morning you will be as bright and cheerful as ever. We should always be gay. Youth is the most joyous season of life, and while we have it we should cultivate a cheerful disposition. Of late, something has passed over you that I could not account for."

"I have felt for a long time as if I should hear something that would make me feel badly."

"There you are, again ; you should banish all such feelings. But come, we will go in now, and you must retire immediately, or else I fear you will be sick to-morrow, and what should I do without you a whole day ?"

Arm in arm the two friends went up to the house. Dora, at the urgent request of Lydia, retired, and in a little while forgot all her troubles ; for no sooner did her head touch the pillow than she was quietly sleeping.

CHAPTER XII.

AUNT NELLY'S DEATH—DORA'S LETTER FROM HER
MOTHER.

WHEN Mrs. M—— wrote to her daughter, Aunt
Nelly was very ill, and from that time commenced
to grow weaker and weaker each day. It was with a
sorrowful heart that Mrs. M—— saw that life was fast
declining. She knew she would lose a much valued
servant, and more than that, she thought of her attachment to Dora. Each day Mrs. M—— gave her her
personal attention, and felt that she could not do too
much, and would have given anything to have her restored to health. She was conscious, however, that her
efforts were vain, for Aunt Nelly was now advanced in
years, and her feeble frame was fast wearing out.

A few mornings previous to her death, Mrs. M——
was talking to her about different things, and in course
of conversation brought up Dora's name. Aunt Nelly
expressed great desire to see her. "Tell her, missus,
dat she mus' meet me in de world ob glory; tell her
dat she mustn't grieve for poor ole Nelly, for she is
gwine to de land of promise. I seed de angels ob glory
last night, an' I knowed dat dey had come for me.
Nelly ain't got long to stay, for she feels dat dis poor
frame ain't gwine to stand much longer. Oh! missus,
if I could only see dat chil' once more. I'se gwine to

meet my little Hannah in heaben, but I would like to see Miss Dora, and tell her good-by, afore I go. Missus, don't forgit to tell her to come to my grave."

Mrs. M—— was much affected to hear her talk; the tears flowed freely, and she knew how grieved Dora would be if she knew how fast Aunt Nelly was sinking.

Mr. M—— came into the cabin to see her. She looked at him intently; at last she spoke: "Massa, I'se gwine to leab yer soon. Nelly ain't long for dis world."

"I have one consolation, Nelly; that is, I know you will soon be in heaven; you have been a faithful servant to me. I offered you your freedom, but you preferred not taking it. I feel better satisfied when I reflect that I offered it to you."

"Massa, you has been mighty good to me; I will be free soon—free from all sorrow. I nebber intended leabing you till de great Massa above sent for me. I will soon go; and den, when Miss Dora comes, she see me no more. Bless dat chil', if I could only see her."

How solemn it was in that cabin now, for death would soon deprive them of one so much loved. All was silence now. Mrs. M—— sat by the bedside, and wept. Aunt Nelly had been with her many years, and now death would separate them. She watched faithfully by the bed—there was no sleep for her now, nor did she grow weary of watching. At times a faint hope that Aunt Nelly would recover, sprang up in her bosom, yet she dare not cherish it; for she well knew that age had weakened her, and that her time had come.

One night Aunt Nelly seemed so much better that Mrs. M—— thought that she might possibly recover. She ate her supper, and seemed to have a much better

appetite than she had had for some time. Mrs. M——
talked to her, and she seemed more cheerful.

But, alas ! it was only a delusion; for about midnight
Aunt Nelly was taken so much worse, that, ere day-
light dawned, her spirit was among the blessed.

Mrs. M—— had been such a constant attendant upon
her that she was quite worn out. They all persuaded
her to lie down and compose herself. Aunt Phebe and
some of the other slaves arranged everything very
properly.

When morning fully dawned, they all set about
arranging matters as well as they could, until Mr.
M—— awoke. The news of Aunt Nelly's death soon
spread throughout the plantation, and all felt deeply
her loss. She was very innocent and unpretending,
and consequently every one loved her.

The next day Aunt Nelly was to be buried. A cler-
gyman was sent for, and she was consigned to the tomb
in a very respectful manner. Mr. M—— gave all the
slaves holiday for the purpose of attending the funeral.
Agreeable to her request, Aunt Nelly was laid by the
side of little Hannah. Mr. M. had a tombstone erected,
with a simple inscription, designating her name, age,
virtues, time of her death, &c.

Mrs. M—— was quite indisposed for several days
after Aunt Nelly's death. She had nursed her quite a
long time, and, not having a very strong constitution,
it was more than she could stand. After she got better,
she wrote to Madora, with a sad heart.

12

" My dear and only Daughter :—

"Perhaps you are impatient at my long silence, but it
was unavoidable. I have been quite indisposed for some days
past, but am now much better. Death has been in our midst,
and taken from us our much loved servant, Aunt Nelly. She
expressed a great desire to see you previous to her death, and I
would that you could have been here. She died quite unexpectedly, indeed ; the night she died we thought she was getting
much better, and entertained hopes of her recovery. But alas !
when we little thought, she breathed her last. Hers was a tri-
umphant death. She has been a faithful servant, and a consciousness that I was kind to her makes me feel more cheerful.
We buried her as she desired, by the side of her little Hannah.
A stone has been erected to her memory. A general gloom has
pervaded the family since her death, and all seem to feel it
deeply. I hope, my dear daughter, that this unwelcome news
will not deter you from your studies. I know that it is calculated to cast a gloom over your joyous spirits, but you must
endeavor to cheer up. You must remember that we cannot live
always, and Aunt Nelly has been in the world a long time, and
it pleased our Father to take her to his bosom. Be consoled
with the idea that she is now in heaven.

"I had a letter from Charles the other day, and he says that
he becomes more and more pleased with the school every day.
He has formed a great many new acquaintances, Aunt Phebe,
Uncle Dick, and all the rest send their best love to you. Your
father left this morning, for the purpose of visiting some of the
other plantations. My love to your friend Lydia, and write often to
                              " Your devoted
                                   " Mother."

Dora's letter was inclosed in a letter to Mrs. P——.
The object of this was to break the subject to Dora in
the best manner possible. So after its reception Mrs.
P—— sent for Dora, and spoke to her of the matter.
Dora felt it keenly, and for a week she scarcely

smiled; indeed, it was some time before she was restored to her former spirits.

"I told you so," said she, one day to Lydia; "I felt it—I knew it. Oh! Lydia, just to think she is dead, and that I will not see her when I go home. Oh! how it grieves me, but I hope it is all for the best. Mamma seems so grieved. Just read the letter."

Dora handed the letter to her, and after she read it, she told her that she should not grieve, for she had gone to a better world.

"I am truly sorry for you, Dora; but you must endeavor to make the best of it, my dear friend. Troubles must come to us all. You have had but few; indeed, they have not as yet commenced."

"Lydia, how can you talk so, when I have just lost one of whom I think so much."

"But, my dear friend, that is a minor trouble, and I hope that you may never know a greater one. I would have you always happy; but then I know sunshine cannot be always—clouds must come over our bright sky; besides, troubles learn us to appreciate blessings more; and if we did not sometimes share them, why then we should not know how to value our blissful moments."

"How you moralize, Lydia. I do wish I could take things just as you do. I dare say I should be much happier if I did."

"I know you would. I am not now blessed with so many luxuries as yourself; but I once knew what it was to share them. My fortune took a reverse step, and that taught me to make the most of everything while I have it."

Madora replied to her mother's letter very shortly

after its reception. She endeavored to write in as cheerful a manner as possible, for she knew how very sad her mother was already. In spite of herself, she would betray her own feelings. She expressed a deep regret at Aunt Nelly's death, and said that she should like to have seen her once more. She spoke of Mrs. P——'s kindness, and the sympathy which she had received from Lydia and the other scholars.

The letter served to cheer Mrs. M—— a little; it was written in rather a different strain from what she expected. She suspected that Dora had disguised her feelings as much as possible, in order to render her more cheerful.

Mr. M—— returned home the day that Dora's letter was received. He noticed with delight how rapidly she was improving, and how beautifully it was dictated; her penmanship was decidedly neat, and she had made rapid progress in that, too.

"I really think," said he to Mrs. M——, "Dora is making great progress. I do not think that we could have done a more advisable thing than sending her to Mrs. P——. That institution has the reputation of being one of the first in the United States, and Dora is amply repaying us for what we are expending upon her education. It will soon be time for the term to close, and I was just thinking where we should take her to recreate."

"Do you not remember that we promised her a visit to Lydia?"

"Oh! sure enough, we did. I had entirely forgotten all about it. Very well; she shall go there, or anywhere she may desire. I would do anything in the world to satisfy her, for she is so dutiful, and all the teachers at the institute give her such a good name. Her birthday will be coming soon, and we must be sure to have something very pretty in readiness for her. I scarcely know what to get. Never mind, we will think of something by that time. I am going to S—— next week, and I expect I shall find something to suit her exactly. I do not care what it costs, I will get it for her. I wish you would write to her to-day, for I do not feel well enough to write myself. Do not mention my indisposition, for she is grieved so much about the death of Aunt Nelly."

"I owe her a letter, so I will write this afternoon. I must write to Charles, too. Have you written to him yet, and informed him of the death of Aunt Nelly?"

"No, I thought of doing so to-day. I shall have to defer it until to-morrow, I think."

It had been some time since Mr. M—— had written to Dora, and he had much to say. He had received a letter from Mr. I——, his Northern friend, and was in anticipation of a visit from him and his family.

"Only think," said Dora, after she read the letter, "papa is going to have a Northern friend to visit him—the gentleman, Lydia, who I told you stopped there about a year ago. I do hope they will defer the visit until it is time for me to go home; I am anxious to see them."

"When does he expect them?"

"Really, I do not know; he did not say in his letter. I suppose it will be some time soon—perhaps in the summer."

"Then I am certain you will not see them; for you know that you are going to make me a visit, and I do not intend to let you get off from it."

"No, indeed; I do not wish to get off from it at all. The last letter that I wrote home, I mentioned the subject to my parents. You know, when they come on to the examination they will have to bring my wardrobe. They will certainly let me go, for you remember the positive promise they made. I hope nothing will prevent me from going."

"Now, just listen at you, Dora; looking on the dark side again. I do not believe I shall ever break you of that habit."

"Oh! I was only jesting. I only said that to see what an effect it would produce on you. You must not mind everything I say."

"Did you not get a letter from your mother to-day?"

"Yes; and she told me to remind you of the promised visit. We will all enjoy ourselves very much, won't we?"

"Yes, indeed; I do wish the time would hurry and come. I know it is sinful to be wishing for time to pass, yet I cannot help it, particularly when I have so much pleasure in the prospective."

"Will your brother return home this vacation?"

"No, he will take a trip somewhere. I do not know what watering-place he designs visiting. So, Dora, you are willing to give up the delightful jaunt to the springs, and go home with me in preference?"

"Yes, indeed; anything to be with you. You know that I shall be in the company of my parents a week at least, and they will not return home until after the vacation, and I shall see them again before they go."

"We shall have a very pleasant time, I know. I live in the city, and you are so fond of gayety; I dare say you will be much delighted."

Dora was full of the thoughts of spending the vacation with Lydia, and was eager for the time to come when she should realize the pleasure she so long anticipated.

CHAPTER XIII.

CHARLES AT COLLEGE—GETS INTO A DIFFICULTY.

WHEN a boy first goes to college, he enters, as it were, into a new world. He sees many new faces, and meets with a diversity of character. He is surrounded by books and instructors. A college life was indeed a novelty to Charles, who had never before been subjected to rules. He knew that he must conform to the regulations of the school, if he wished to gain the good-will and approbation of his tutors.

At the time of which we are now speaking he had been at college twelve months, and had become accustomed to what he thought at first very strange, and he found that there was nothing like getting used to things.

Charles was naturally very ambitious, and studied assiduously every lesson assigned him.

"Oh!" thought he, "what a long and tedious time it will be before I complete my studies. But I must not give up, for I can never take the second step until I take the first. I must endeavor to press on."

With this thought he would feel a little encouraged, and determined in his own mind to accomplish everything that he undertook.

When a student applies himself diligently, and shows that he is endeavoring to conform strictly to the rules of the college, his instructors do not allow it to pass unnoticed. No, no; often a kind word is offered to impel him onward.

It seems that Charles was quite a favorite with the students and instructors; and though the latter would make no positive demonstration of it, yet he could easily see that they had a high regard for him. It is strictly against the regulations of a college to exhibit any signs of partiality whatever, for it is so apt to produce unpleasant feelings among the pupils. One day Charles was sent for by Professor C——. He had noticed for some time that he seemed to be trying to do his duty, and thought he would give him some word by way of encouragement.

"Well, Charles, how are you progressing in your studies? I see that you are applying yourself, and I hope that you will meet with great success."

Charles colored a little as he replied: "I was thinking the other day what a long time it would be before I should complete my college course, and it seemed like a tedious period, indeed."

"You must not feel discouraged, Charles, nor think of the length of time—only to improve as much as possible. You know that we ascend the Hill of Science step by step. It is, indeed, very gradual; but, with proper attention to study, we shall reach the summit after all our trouble. Take good care that you do not pause to look back as you ascend, lest you should fall before you reach the top. I suppose you like the studies you have?".

"O yes, sir; only I would like to be in higher ones. I see some of my comrades studying in much higher classes than I."

" But you must remember that they have been here much longer than yourself, and are older. The rudiments must be learned first, and then the higher branches. You know that A, B, C had to be learned before you could read. Our greatest men had to learn step by step, and see what a name they have acquired —a name that will ever live in memory. I think that, so far, you are in a fair way to get in higher classes very soon; and I sincerely hope that your deportment will always be such as it has been in past time, and that you will study with the same zeal. Go now, Charles, impressed with what I have said to you; and whenever you feel discouraged, or think that others are in higher classes than yourself, remember that they had to learn the minor branches before they could undertake the greater ones."

Oh! how beautiful is the dream of ambition to the young student who endeavors to make progress. He thinks of the laurels and the name he will win. In imagination, he sees his name carved on the pinnacles of fame, and a thousand followers at his feet. He looks forward to the time when his name and honor will be proclaimed throughout the world. Such were the thoughts of Charles. He had always loved to read, from his earliest years, and particularly of great men, and he often desired to become thus renowned. He knew what a pleasure it would afford his parents when he should have returned home crowned with honor; and the thoughts, too, of meeting his sister, whose absence had rendered her more dear.

For a time all things went on very smoothly. But

sometimes, in spite of all our endeavors, something will occur to mar it all.

There happened to be two boys, much larger and older than Charles, at college, who were extremely reckless; they paid no attention whatever to the rules of the college or studies. They had noticed Charles frequently, and knew that he was quite a favorite among the instructors, so they determined to do something which would cause him trouble. One day they were bent on going fishing. There was a pond near, and sometimes the boys would go, though it was positively against the orders of the instructors for them to go fishing there. The two boys, however, had determined upon going, and to involve Charles in a difficulty.

"Well, boys," said one, "let us play a nice trick upon that chickenhearted fellow, who is always so afraid of the teachers; for my part, I don't care for any of them; if they choose to expel me they are welcome; I don't care at all."

"What shall we do?" asked John; "we shall have to tell a very straight tale to him; you know he would not go without asking the teachers. For my part, I wish he was tied to old Professor C——, and had to stay there until he left college. But say, what shall we contrive; what sort of a trap shall we make to catch him in?"

"I'll tell you; I will just go to him, and ask him if he does not want to go fishing; if he says that he will go ask the professor, I will tell him that I will go. You know he thinks that everybody is like himself, and will do all they promise. I will pretend as if I have obtained permission, and we must be all ready to start that minute, lest he should become dubious."

"Agreed," said the other; "Will, you are a capital hand at anything of this sort. But you will have to pretend that a great many other boys are going, for you know that he would not go with us alone. You can say, 'Come, go with us, Charlie, the rest will follow;' or we will pretend that they have all gone."

Off goes Will, as he was called at college, to search for Charles. He had a great many ways of getting around people by his smooth words, and pretending to do so much. He found Charles studying his Latin lesson, sitting under a tree. He ran up to him, and commenced talking.

"I see you are studying hard yet; well, it is always the case with you; I declare, I believe you are the most studious fellow in school. You must not injure your health by studying too hard, for then you know that it would not be of any service to you in after life. I think it is all very right and proper to study our lessons well, but then I believe in recreation. I do not remember of having seen you on the play-ground to-day."

"No," replied Charles; "I have been busy preparing this Latin lesson. You know I have been studying Latin for a year, and I am anxious now to get in some higher book than Cæsar."

"But you must not study so much; it will ruin your health, and break down your constitution."

"I am very much obliged to you, William, for the interest you take in me, and I believe I will shut the book up, and take a little recreation."

" That is the most advisable thing you can do. Suppose we go on a little excursion to the fishing-pond this afternoon, it is not far?"

" We must first get permission from the instructors."

" Certainly we must, Charles; I did not think of going without, and if you will just wait here, I will run and ask him. Give me your book, and I will take it to your room for you. I know the professor will consent to let us go, for there are so many other boys going. They have gone, I believe, by this time. You can go along with John and myself. I am going to get leave; wait till I come back."

Will then ran off at full speed (as he pretended) to ask the professor. He met John, and with a meaning laugh said: " We've got him now, and I guess when he gets back, he will feel the worse for it. You ought just to have heard how nicely I got around him; he agreed to let me ask permission of Professor C——. We will stop and talk awhile before I go back, or he might suspect."

" You must keep a very straight face, for if you were to laugh, he might think that something was wrong directly. I think we had better hurry, for it is getting late, and then he will say it is getting night, and we had better not go."

There were several ponds around, and the boys thought they would select the farthest one, and go the most winding way possible, so that Charles would have to wait until they came home, before he could come.

" Are you all ready to go, Charles?" said Will, " if so, come along; we shall all have a nice time, I know."

" You have obtained permission to go, then?"

13

"O yes; and all the rest have gone by this time."
The boys all started for the pond.

"Where are the other boys?" asked Charles, looking around, and not seeing any except Will and John.

"Oh! I expect they have gone to the other pond;
we don't always go to the same one. But never mind,
we shall enjoy ourselves the more as there is no one
else here."

They stayed for some time, and it was getting late;
the sun had set, and in a very little while it would be
night.

"We had better return, now," said Charles; "indeed, we are staying too late; it will never do; it will
never do for us to take advantage of liberty given us,
in this way."

"Oh! taking advantage," said Will and John; "I
guess you will have to learn all these things, before you
are here much longer."

"But I do not wish to learn them. I am ambitious
to regard the rules of the school, and I am sure I shall
be much happier by so doing; it is only when we do our
best that we escape trouble."

"Well, as for my part," said Will, "I go along just
so; and I find that I do as well as any one. If I violate the rules, I do it in such a manner as not to be
found out."

"That is very wrong, indeed; and you ought to
remember that if the instructors do not see us, God
does."

"Come, do not preach a sermon. I think we had
as well go now as not, for it is getting dark; it will be
candlelight by the time we get back."

"Where are those boys?" asked one of the professors, in a reproving voice; "I thought it was about time for them to commence their old ways again. I supposed that suspension from college would have taught them a lesson, but I see they have forgotten it. I will certainly expel them, for I find that it is no use to put up with them any longer."

"Charles M——, Charles M——," said another; "I wonder where he is. Surely, he could not have gone with them. I thought better of him than to think he would violate the rules thus. I find, after all, that appearances will deceive. Can any one of the students tell me where he is?"

"I saw him in company with Will L—— and John F—— this afternoon," said one of the students. "I heard them say something about going to the fishing-pond. I think they all three went together."

"Is it possible that they have gone to that pond again? I gave all the students express orders not to go. I will make them all answer for it; and I dare say it will not be forgotten soon, either."

About candlelight, in came the three boys. Who should they meet but the professor!

"Go to my room sir," said he to Charles.

What to make of this abrupt speaking, he knew not. "What have I done?" thought he. He dreaded to see the professor enter the room, although he could think of nothing to get punished for, unless it was staying so late at the pond, and that was not his fault.

In a few minutes the professor entered.

"I never thought this of you, Charles," said he. "Here you have been staying at this late hour; you knew very well that it was time for you to be at your studies. I am afraid that I shall have to resort to harsh means if you will not obey in any other way."

"I did not mean to stay so late," replied Charles (not knowing that no permission had been given to go), it was not my fault. I wanted to come before, but I could not find the way, and the boys would not show me. I begged them to come."

"That is no excuse at all, sir. Go to your room, and to-morrow morning, when I send for the others, you come too."

It was the first time that Charles had met the professor without receiving a smile from him. Oh! how heavy was his heart that night; how he wept, and thought of his mother and sister. He could not get asleep for some time, and, when he did, he dreamed of the pond and the frowning looks of the professor.

The next morning all three of the boys were sent for; and now, with looks of fear, they entered the room. Charles was the first one whom he addressed.

"I wish to know," said he, "what led you to go to the fishing-pond?"

"I had permission to go, or I should never have thought of going."

"Who gave it to you?"

"Will and John said that you gave us permission, and with that I went. I should not break a rule on any consideration whatever, if I knew it. I have always endeavored to please the instructors in every possible way."

"It was not your fault, then, that you went to the pond?"

"No, sir."

"You were under the impression that I had given permission for you all to go?"

"Yes, sir."

"So you are at the bottom of it all," he said, turning to Will and John. "I thought it very strange that Charles, who has been so very exemplary, should go to a place which I so often have forbidden the students going to. I intend to expel you both from college the very next time that you violate the rules of school in such a perverse manner. I think you deserve it now, and am almost ready to make up my mind not to let you stay here another day; for I feel that I am doing the college an injustice to allow two such reckless boys to stay here. If I do not see a very great change for the better, I shall most certainly resort to expulsion. Go now to your studies, and be very careful how you conduct yourselves, or else abide by the consequences."

After the two boys left the room, the professor told Charles that he was very sorry he had been deceived by those two boys; that he had not given them any permission at all to go; they had not even asked him.

He added farther, that he had caught them in an untruth, and hoped he would beware of them in future.

"It is the first time, Charles," said he, "that I have ever given you a cross look, and I am glad to find that it was not deserved. You were deceived by those reckless boys, who pay no attention whatever to rules. You must be more careful in future."

Now, with a kind smile from the professor, and a light heart, Charles went to his studies. Ever after that he was more careful, and avoided the company of

13*

Will and John, for he feared lest they should get him into another difficulty. He saw very plainly what bad company would do, and thought it best to shun them altogether. It was much to his advantage, too, that he did, for shortly afterwards the two boys were expelled from college.

Charles was happy to think he had got out of the difficulty, and that if he had met the frowning looks of the professor once, they were not merited; and he determined in his own mind to be always on the "look out" hereafter.

CHAPTER XIV.

BENJAMIN AND HIS MASTER.

"WELL, Benjamin, what is the matter this morning? You look as smiling and cheerful as possible; something is in the wind, I dare say. Well, out with it, and we will see what can be done."

"Massa, does yer hab any recollection ob dat ar' Lizzie, what missus got to hope her, when Miss Dora wa' gwine 'way ter school?"

"Well, what of her, Benjamin?"

"Why, massa, I was tinking 'bout how I would like to ax' her to hab me; but den she libs on de tor'er plantation, you know de one what Mr. B—— libs on. He talks how he 'spects ter go 'way soon, and den you know Liz will hab ter go too."

"I am sorry for you, Benjamin; but we will see what can be done for you."

Benjamin, it seems, had become much infatuated with Lizzie, or Liz, as he called her. He knew, however, that it would never do to marry her, because he would have to be separated from her. Ben thought that he would go and see what his master would do; he knew very well that he was kind and indulgent, and would do anything to please his slaves.

Ben was quite delighted with the answer his master had made him, and now began to build many air-castles.

He thought perhaps his master would buy her, and then they never should be parted; for he had often heard his master say that he was opposed to separating any slave from his wife.

Mr. M—— pondered, and thought which would be best to do. Finally, he concluded to set Benjamin free; buy Lizzie, and set her free. He thought he would see what Mrs. M—— said, before he spoke to Ben.

"I have been thinking," said he to Mrs. M——, "what would be the best thing I could do. Ben came to see me one day, and gave me to understand that he was anxious to marry that girl you had here to help you sew, when Dora was going to school."

"Well, I thought he seemed to be quite attentive, but I did not notice it very particularly. What is the plan you thought of?"

"I was thinking that I would give Ben his freedom, and then buy Lizzie, and set her free."

"I think that would do very well. Ben has been such a faithful slave; I think he has conducted himself very properly; and I think you might give it to him. We have enough without him. If he chooses, you might let him have the cabin so long as he pleases to stay. You had better ascertain first, however, whether Mr. B—— would sell Lizzie; for if you were to mention the subject to Ben it would raise his exultations too high, and he might be disappointed."

"That is very true; I will not say anything, but ride over to the plantation immediately."

No sooner said than done; Mr. M—— went to Mr. B——'s plantation, and found him at home.

"I have come," said he, "to know if you will sell me your servant, the one they call Lizzie."

"Well! I do not like the idea of selling my slaves; but if you will tell me your object, and she desires to go, I will sell her to you; for I know that you are very kind to your slaves, and I dare say she will be as well taken care of as she is here."

"My object, sir, is simply this: I have a servant, Ben; I suppose you have seen him?"

"O yes; the one who plays on the banjo so much."

"The same. He came to me the other evening, looking very smilingly indeed. Said I, 'Ben, what is the matter?' He told me he had formed a great attachment for your servant, and asked me what he should do. He said you were going away, and he would have to be separated from her. I told him that I would see what could be done. I thought to buy Lizzie, and set her free with Ben."

"Well, I have no objections, now that I see what your object is. I will speak to her, and let you know to-morrow."

"Very well. I bid you good-day."

After Mr. M—— had gone, he spoke to his wife upon the subject; and she told him that, if Lizzie had no objections, he might sell her to Mr. M——. She knew that she had a great attachment for Ben, and she was going away; then, if she carried Lizzie with her, they would be separated.

Mrs. B—— was very humane. She revolted at the idea of selling slaves away from their husbands, wives, or children. She determined to let Mr. M—— have Lizzie, if she desired it.

"Lizzie," said she, "Mr. M—— has been here, and wishes to know if I will sell you to him. I suppose you know the reason?"

"Lors bless me, missus, dat I do, for his Ben wants to marry me; but den he tought dat you would be gwine 'way, and dat he would hab to leab me."

"Are you willing to go?"

"I'se mighty sorry, 'deed, to part wid you, missus; but den I lubs dat ar' Ben—an' don't he play on de banjo doe? I do tink dat ar' nigger beats all I eber seed."

With this Lizzie began to dance, imagining that she heard Ben playing on the banjo.

"You are willing to go, Lizzie?"

"Yes, marm."

"I'll tell you what I will do; I did not think of it before. I thought I would sell you at first, but now I think very differently. I will give you your freedom."

"Den kin I go to Ben, missus?"

"Certainly you can."

"Will Mr. M—— gib Ben hizzen?"

"Yes, that is just what he is going to do."

"Well, what did Lizzie say about this matter?" asked Mr. B—— of his wife, after the interview which she had with Lizzie.

"Oh! she is very willing to go. It is true she regrets leaving me, but then you know how it is; her affections are centered upon Ben, and it is perfectly natural that she should wish to go."

"I thought that I would not sell her, but would give her her freedom. What say you?"

"That is just what I said this morning to her. She is delighted with the idea."

"I will go over and inform Mr. M——. I told him that I would let him know this afternoon."

Mr. B—— made all possible haste to inform Mr. M—— of his intentions regarding the servant.

"I spoke to her this morning, and I think, from what she told me, that Ben has said something to her about it. She is very willing to go."

"I'se gwine to ax' massa dis berry day, and see what he's gwine to do 'bout Lizzie, so I kin tell her what he says on Saturday night, when I goes over to play for dem dar niggers to dance. Since I got my new banjo, dey wants me to be playing for dem all de time."

"What's dat yer is gwine to ax' massa 'bout?" asked Aunt Phebe, who was standing near.

"I wants to get married to dat ar' Miss Lizzie, and I ax'd massa de tother day what he was gwine to do."

"What did he say?"

"Well, he told me dat he mighty sorry, and he would see what he could do for me."

"You had better go and ax' him now, I tink, for I jist seed him go in de house; he might go off somewhar', and den you wouldn't see him for a week."

Ben went accordingly, to hear what his case would be.

"Massa, how yer do, sir, to-day?"

"I am very well, Ben; how are you?"

"Oh! berry well, 'deed. Massa, I came to ax' yer 'bout dat matter now, what I spoke to yer 'bout de tother day."

"Well, Ben, I have pleasant news to tell you. Mr. B—— says that he will set Lizzie free, and I am going to set you free; so you see you can be married after all, can't you."

"Yes, sar, massa; but den, if I is sot free, I won't hab to leab yer, will I?"

"No, indeed, Ben; I will let you live in that little cabin as long as you wish to, and behave yourself."

"Berry well, massa; but den I don't like de idee of being free."

"Why not?"

"'Caze den I is afeared dat yer won't care nuffin' for me, den."

O yes, I will; do not fear anything of the sort. I will care as much for you then as I do now."

"Den massa, if yer say dat I may stay wid yer all de time, den I will hab my freedom."

"Yes, Ben; you know that I told you you might stay on the plantation, and live in the cabin you now have. You can work for yourself. Your mistress often needs some one to assist her, so she can give employment to your wife that is to be. I think with these prospects you can get along very well. I will see that you want for nothing."

"Tank you, sar, massa; I will tell her all 'bout dat when I sees her."

One can easily imagine the delight which Ben experienced on the reception of that welcome news from his master. He went to Aunt Phebe's cabin, to tell her; it seems that she was the first one they all went to, to communicate any intelligence.

Aunt Phebe said that she wondered what "massa was gwine to do next?" and that she "never heerd of so many weddins in all her life afore," and that she didn't care nuffin' 'bout it, nohow; dey all might git married if dey pleased. Now dar's anudder job for Phebe to do; bake de cakes. Well, I don't care, 'caze I will git my share, anyhow."

Never was Saturday so long coming before. Ben thought it never would come.

Early the next evening (which was Saturday), he went over to convey the intelligence to Lizzie. She was perfectly delighted; indeed, it would be difficult to tell which seemed the most pleased, Lizzie or Ben.

"Well, Lizzie ('scuse me for not calling you Miss), we will have a weddin' purty soon, and den we will hab de banjo 'gin. Well, I wonders who is gwine to play de banjo? Nebber mind, I don't care, 'caze I can do 'dout dancin', anyhow. If I don't play, den dey wouldn't hab any fun. I do wonder what all dem dar black niggers will say when it comes off."

It was agreed upon that the wedding should come off .very shortly, and everything was to be prepared as nicely as possible.

"Well," said Rufus to Laura, "hab you heerd anyting 'bout dat weddin' what is gwine to come off soon?"

"No; what weddin' is it?"

"Why, dat ar' Ben, what busts de banjo playing on it; he is gwine to git married to dat 'ar Liz, what comed here and hoped missus, when Miss Dora was gwine 'way. I seed dem fixing up dat cabin mighty nice, and I tought den dat dar was somefing in de wind."

"Well, I hopes dey will be happy," said Laura,

14

"and I am glad dat she is comin', for it will be great company for me."

"You ought jist hab seen dem together de tother Sunday. I nebber seed such 'fectation in all my life; dar Liz was, flinging her head back, and you nebber did see such airs in all your life; dar she was, larfin' and capering dar, afore Ben, and she did look jist like a fool."

" I'se mighty glad dat dar will be a weddin', 'caze I wants to go to one, I tell you. How long afore it come off?"

"Berry soon, so I heerd 'em say; I heerd Aunt Phebe talking to Uncle Dick 'bout de cakes, and dat's how I knowed anyting 'bout it."

" Who gwine to play de banjo, for 'em to dance?"

" Why, Ben, sure; he ain't got no notion ob habin' de weddin', and den no dancin'. I must hab dem ar' boots cleaned up, and dat ar' collar stiffened. I 'spects Aunt Phebe will sputter 'nough, when I axes her 'bout doing it."

Rufus's greatest ambition was to have a collar as stiff and as high as possible, no matter how much inconvenience it put him to; he prided himself upon tight boots, and it made no difference whether the remainder of the dress corresponded or not.

Laura commenced to think of what she should wear, and looked over her wardrobe, selecting, of course, the most gorgeous dressing she had.

It was near Christmas, too! On a Southern plantation this season of festivity is looked forward to with much delight. Each slave always expects some little present from their owners, who never fail to remember them.

Some of the slaves were getting their chickens ready to take to market; others were cutting celery; while others were preparing mince-meat, and making all possible preparations for Christmas.

Ben thought that he would defer the wedding till then, for he knew that his master intended making him a present of a handsome suit of clothes; and besides, he thought they would all have a jolly time, as it was a general holiday for all the slaves.

"Lizzie," said Mrs. B—— one day, "it is only two weeks to Christmas, and you will then be married. You will of course have to leave me to go on Mr. M——'s plantation. I am very sorry to give you up, and would not do so if you did not desire it. I gave you your freedom because, if I had sold you, you would have thought that I cared more for the money than I did for you, and would sell you just to get it."

"Lah! missus, I knowed better dan dat."

"Well, you might not have thought so, possibly, but others would. I wish you to prepare for your wedding. I have several new dresses, which I purchased for you as a present; the white one is to be worn on the night you are married. As I leave next week, and do not care to be troubled with carrying away any more things than I can avoid, I thought I would leave you the carpet which is on my chamber, and one or two quilts. When I leave you, I do not want you to forget me. Remember that I only permitted you to leave me because it was your choice. I sincerely hope that

you may ever be treated kindly, and have no doubt but
what you will, if you conduct yourself in a becoming
manner."

Lizzie was much affected at what her mistress had
said to her, and felt very sad, indeed, at parting with
her.   She knew, however, that she was free, and, in
case of any emergency, she could return to her mistress,
who would always willingly offer her a home.

Two weeks passed, Christmas came, and a gay time
it was; every family in the cabins was busy.   Aunt
Phebe had been occupied some·time making mince-
meat; now she was roasting turkeys, chickens, &c.   In
her oven were mince-pies, lemon-puddings, and various
other kinds of pastry.

Mr. M—— had invited quite a number of persons to
dine there, and among the number were Mr. and Mrs.
B——.   In the evening, the great wedding was to come
off, and the slaves were looking forward to the time with
much pleasure.   Ben was tuning up his banjo, and trying
it, to see how it would sound.   Lizzie was arranging the
dressing which she intended to wear on the occasion.

Mrs. M—— had a table nicely furnished with all
kinds of dainties, and the evening passed off delight-
fully; and we will venture to say that this Christmas
season was long remembered by all on the plantation.

The cabin in which the newly-married couple were to
live was all neatly furnished.   Ben did not look at the
carpet without smiling, and told Lizzie that she need
not mind about saving up the rags now.for a carpet,
for they had got a "splendiferous" one, and such a one
as never before graced the plantation.

Aunt Phebe was very busy for about a week, making pies and cakes to send Dora. Mrs. M—— always sent her those things at Christmas, as a present from Aunt Phebe; and she showed how highly they were appreciated by the manner in which they were made way with. Dora always boasted about Aunt Phebe's pies and cakes, and she now had a fair chance to show her schoolmates what kind of pies Aunt Phebe could make, and they all agreed in pronouncing them decidedly good.

14*

CHAPTER XV.

DORA'S VISIT TO LYDIA—THE RAMBLE—THE DEPARTURE.

"NEW ENGLAND, New England, my happy home! How my heart leaps with joy to think that I once more behold thee. Earth hath many bright spots, but none so fair as this. 'Tis here my forefathers bore many hardships; and now, as I stand upon this hallowed land, I feel that I love none like thee. I would not give thee up for the far-famed isles of the sea, where an eternal spring pervades. No, no; give me the 'snow-clad hills' of my own dear home; I am far happier here than I could be anywhere on earth. Now, after the toils of school-days, I recreate, and breathe again the air of my loved home."

Thus soliloquized Lydia, as she stood by an open window and looked upon the beautiful scenery around. She thought that no spot on earth could vie with it in loveliness. She saw the flowers all beautifully painted with divers colors, and watched the limpid stream as it leaped onward. She heard the carolling of birds, and humming of insects. She thought of what Dora had said about her home at the "sunny South," and felt that it could not surpass her own.

It was summer, when nature puts on its gayest livery. Vacation had come at last, and the long-looked for time when Dora was to accompany her home.

Dora could scarcely realize that she was so far away from her "sunny home."

"Oh!" exclaimed Dora, a day or two after she arrived at Lydia's, "what a charming place, dear friend. I had an idea that in New England it was so cold and chilling; I even imagined that it could not be pleasant in the summer time. How agreeably disappointed I am in the place. I would not have missed the trip for anything in the world."

"I am delighted to think that you are so pleased, and hope that you will continue thus. I know if lovely scenes in nature can make you happy, you will be pleased here."

"Is it not delightful to come to a place like this, after having studied so long? It is such charming recreation. When you first mentioned my going home with you, I did not expect to come; I always thought it such a long distance; but I am here at last. I do wonder what Aunt Phebe would say to it? Talk enough about it, I will wager."

"Hark! I hear a carriage, and it seems to be very near. I wonder who it can be," said Lydia. "Oh! it is brother. Now, what a teaze he is; he pretended that he should not be home for a week or two. How he loves to surprise any one. Well, I am heartily glad he has come. The carriage has stopped; I am going to meet him. Come with me, Dora."

"No, Lydia, I can't go now. You know that I have but a slight acquaintance with him."

"Well, you will excuse me for a few minutes, won't you?"

"Certainly."

" Then I will go and meet him."

Lydia had kept it a secret from Harry that Dora would accompany her home; she wanted to take him by surprise. She thought that it would be something quite unlooked for.

After he had been home a little while, Lydia told him that she had a visitor.

" A visitor! How long has she been here?"

" About four or five days."

" Where is she, that she does not appear?"

" Oh! she will be visible after a while."

" Do tell me who she is."

" Wait a while; I want to keep you in suspense."

Lydia went up stairs and told Dora what conversation had passed between her and her brother.

" I dare say he will be much surprised when he sees the Niagara lady."

In a little while the two girls made their appearance, and who should the visitor be but Dora, the young lady whom he had met at the Falls."

Harry was perfectly thunderstruck, and withal very much delighted.

" Well, really, Miss Dora, I did not anticipate meeting you here, or I would have hurried home. I did not travel hastily, I took my time, and it has been a week since I left college. I have, I am happy to say, completed my course of study. It is, indeed, a gratification to me when I think of it, for a college life is certainly not a very desirable one."

Since Harry had met Dora at the Falls, she had been the idol of his dreams. He had thought of her as some gentle spirit reared in a southern clime, and saw beauty in her every feature. Now that he had returned from college, crowned with honors, bright hopes for the future filled his mind. He determined on attaining a zenith of glory; and, when that was accomplished, he would be happy.

He was anxious to render Dora's visit as agreeable as possible, and he was not wanting, by any means, in gallantry. It was his chief delight to take her riding or walking. Often he would go with his sister and Dora into the woods, and they would gather wild flowers; with them he would twine a wreath, and place it upon Dora's brow, as an emblem of the laurels with which he hoped some day to be crowned. Dora played most exquisitely upon the guitar; she had an uncommon talent for music, and her voice was admirably adapted either for the piano or guitar. Often Harry and Dora would go at evening's hour and sit upon the rocks by the water's edge, and Dora would play her most plaintive and touching airs; it would seem as though an angel were passing its fingers over the chords. Harry would look first upon the glassy stream at his feet, and then upon the lovely being before him. He listened, and was enchanted with the echo of the chords touched by the fingers of Dora; he watched her curls, which were gently kissed by the passing zephyr. Lydia, too, gazed upon her, and thought her more beautiful than ever. She was like some fair rose bursting into beauty; its tints do not surpass that of her own cheek, for even now it glowed with radiance as she sang so sweetly, and gave full expression to every word which she uttered.

The days passed on rapidly, much to the regret of Lydia, for she would gladly have prolonged the time,

which, a month or two since, she would have shortened.
But school-hours always pass on more heavily than
those at home. Dora became more and more pleased
every day, and she thought New England almost as
lovely as her own dear home.

"It is near time, Dora," said Lydia one day, "for
us to return to school again. I do dread the idea of
returning again. It does seem to me that I never passed
a more delightful vacation. How brief, too, it has been
to me; it seems but yesterday that the examination
closed, and now we are doomed to return to the old accustomed place."

"I never expect to see this lovely spot again, Lydia.
I feel such a reluctance, too, in leaving it. I almost
wish I had never come, for it will always pain me to
think of it."

"I sincerely hope, my dear friend, that this is not
your last visit to me. I should feel very sad, indeed, if
I thought it was. Do you not expect us to continue our
friendship after we leave school? It would be worth-
less, indeed, if it were to exist only so long as school-
days lasted."

"I did not mean to say that our friendship would not
still exist; I was thinking of the distance we lived
apart; and you know, my dear friend, that many changes
take place in life ; some of them are very sad, too."

"I hope that yours, dear Dora, will ever be a sunny
existence, as it is now."

Harry had been listening to the conversation, and
was waiting for an opportunity to speak.

"I hope, Miss Dora, that you are not endeavoring
to impress us with the idea that you will not visit us

again; we should feel that we had not rendered your visit agreeable. I shall certainly expect to see you here again."

Dora little knew what was passing in his mind; she knew not his dream of happiness for the future. He had many beautiful visions before his view, and he thought some day to be happy in the realization of them.

She replied by saying that she hoped to see that place again, for it had many dear associations for her.

" I am delighted to find that you will think of it with so much pleasure."

" I shall ever remember it, and wish to pay it another visit; but I must hope for the best."

The last day, the last hour, the last minute must come for all things; and although we are so reluctant to give up our joys, yet we must do so.

The last day came that Lydia was to remain at home for the present.

Oh! how the two girls felt when they saw the sun peering through the window, for they well knew that the next time those bright rays were seen, they would be on their way to school.

" Well, Dora, this is our last morning here; you know that we start this afternoon for R——. Oh! I do wish we could only stay a week longer; I think I would endeavor to make more of my time. Really, it has passed away so swiftly; if it only glided away thus pleasantly at school, we should not mind staying; but there is a vast difference between school and home;

really, I feel so much at home here, that when I speak of it I always say home."

"I am sad indeed, dear Lydia, to part from New England; it does seem to me, that somehow, by magic, I have become so much infatuated with it."

"Would you like to change it for your own?"

"O no; I love my own home too well to wish to give it up. If you were to go there once, I dare say you would be as much infatuated as I am with your home. Just go to the magnolia vale when the sun is setting, and inhale the rich fragrance; I know that you would never wish to leave it. You have heard of the South, I dare say, but then you can know nothing of its charms until you visit there."

"Well, I hope to go there, some time," said Harry. "The breakfast-bell is ringing; it is the last one for us here, for awhile, at least."

"I believe this is the last day for you to remain here. Really, I wish that you could prolong your visit. I do believe time has passed on more rapidly, just to teaze us," said Harry, laughingly.

"It does seem so to me. I can scarcely realize that I have been here two whole months; but it is true."

"You leave this afternoon."

"Yes," said Lydia.

"I have a great notion to accompany you all to school, if 'pa will give up his trip."

"O do," said Lydia. "I know we shall all have such a charming time; what a happy trio it would be. Do you not second it, Dora?"

"By all means; Mr. B——, we will be delighted to

have your company; the only disadvantage is, it will render our trip so much shorter."

"I believe that in travelling, generally persons are anxious to get to the end of their journey as quick as possible."

"Well, so it may be, under some circumstances; but when they have agreeable company, they like to be as long about it as they can."

During the morning they were very busy packing up, and arranging everything for their departure.

How different was their departure to their preparation for going home. Indeed, they put each dress in with reluctance, and could they have followed their own inclinations, they would have left them out a month longer.

"What a nice description I shall have to give Aunt Phebe. I know she will ask me a thousand questions; she has such an aversion to the North."

"Well, you find that many persons at the South have a dislike for the North."

"I will tell Aunt Phebe all about it, when I go home."

"I do not believe that Aunt Phebe will scarcely know you, Dora, for you have altered so much. When you first came North you were so pale, but now your complexion has quite a rosy hue."

"I know Aunt Phebe will not believe it until she sees me."

"You will then have a very agreeable surprise for her."

"I dare say it will be. It will take me a month to

15

answer all the questions that she will put to me. O, I forgot to tell you, Lydia, and it happened quite a long time ago. You remember Ben, of whom you have heard me speak so often? He was a great one for playing on the banjo—he is married now, and his wife and himself are both free. I dare say they are a happy couple. He married the sempstress whom 'ma employed to help get me ready when I was going to R——. She is quite pretty, I think; I remember that she had quite a pretty figure, very tall and slender. A great many changes have taken place since I left home."

"Yes, quite a number; but none of them are very serious, excepting the death of Aunt Nelly. But I will not speak of that, for it always makes me so sad when I think of it. When do you expect to return home, Dora?"

"In about two years."

"That is not a very great way off."

"Well, I think it will appear a very long time to me. You know how very monotonous school-life is; there is but little variation, if any. But I shall not have so much time to think of home next term, for I am going to study Spanish and German, and it will occupy much of my time. I am anxious to make quite a progress by the time I leave; and, in order to do so, I shall have to study quite hard. I have but one regret to make, dear Lydia, and that is a sad one, too."

"What is it, Dora?"

"You know, my friend, that this is the last term for you to be at school. Just to think, I shall have to return all by myself. If this were my senior year, I know that time would appear shorter, for I should have so many more studies to occupy my mind, and I should cease to think of home so often."

" That time will come for you—soon come for you; only one more year, and then you will have finished! Your brother will complete the year before you, does he not?"

" Yes; and I often think how delighted my parents will be, if he acquits himself well."

" That he will do, I have no doubt."

" I hope so, at least."

" We will go out, Dora, and take a little ramble this morning; it will serve to amuse us, and I suppose you would like to give the wild-flowers a farewell smile. There comes Harry, and he will go with us. I have no doubt but what he has come to invite us; do not let us say a word; we will see what his intentions are."

"Well, young ladies, what have you on the programme for the morning? I think a walk will be a pleasant amusement; what do you say? The weather is fine, and I dare say it will prove very beneficial to you both; and, besides, it will afford me much pleasure."

" We were just anticipating a walk; we saw you coming, and thought we would hear what you had to say."

" I have come in good time, then."

" Exactly," replied both.

" We had better start now, or it will be getting dinner time. You know we all leave at five o'clock this afternoon."

" Oh! do not speak of leaving."

" It is equally as disagreeable for me to think of it

as yourselves, but you know it must be; sometimes we have to do things very contrary to our wishes."

"It is a charming morning," said Lydia, as they walked on; "I declare, it seems a pity that we are compelled to leave here just at the time when everything is most beautiful. Just see the flowers, how lovely! They appear sad this morning; I expect they are mourning our departure. Here is the very spot where you sat last evening, Miss Dora, and played upon the guitar; do you not remember? What a beautiful night it was, and how charmed I was at your music! I shall never walk here, never look upon that rock, but what I shall think of the time, and the one who sang there."

"I am glad you have something wherewith to remember me."

"Oh! it would not need anything to call you to mind; but then this rock will seem to have a voice whenever I pass it."

"Here is a spring, Lydia; now for a drink of water. I wish the water possessed the same virtues as the spring which lay at the foot of Parnassus; that, you know, inspired all with knowledge who drank of its waters."

"I heartily wish, then, that we might come across it in our travels."

"What shall we do for something to drink out of? We have no cup."

"Stop," said Harry, "I will get one of those large leaves. You shall not be at a loss for a cup."

"Oh! how cool and delightful this water is."

"Well, I must say good-by to the spring, for I

never expect to see it again. I fancy I hear the leaves and flowers whisper 'farewell.' I do wish I had my guitar here, I would sing a requiem to them."

"Oh! would it not be delightful?" said Harry; "really, I do wish you had brought it with you.".

"It must be getting late," said Dora, looking up at the sun; "its shadows are getting longer. I think we should begin to make our way homeward; you know I did not finish packing my trunk."

Slowly and reluctantly did they wend their steps towards the house; they felt as though they were treading upon hallowed ground. But, alas! Lydia was compelled to leave her dear home. That evening, ere the sun should set, she would be many miles away from fair New England's shore.

15*

CHAPTER XVI.

MR. I——'S VISIT TO THE SOUTH.

WE will pass over a space of about two years, since Mr. I——'s visit to the South. He had not forgotten the hospitality which he had met, and often felt a desire to renew it.

As it happened, that summer he was compelled to go South, having some particular business with the cotton merchants. He thought he would start much earlier than usual, so as to have an opportunity of making a nice visit to Mr. M——. He had received so many very pressing invitations to come and bring his wife, that he was determined to accept.

"Mrs. I——," said he to his wife, "you can get ready for our trip South, for it will be a very short time before we leave."

"Really, I do not know what to do about going South; for I dislike the idea so much of being among slaveholders. I am afraid my visit will not prove agreeable. What arrangement have you made?"

"I thought I would take you to my friend Mr. M——'s, and then go on and attend to my business engagements; and when I got through, I would call for you. Does it accord with your wishes?"

"It depends upon how long you intend staying. What if I do not like the place? then I should be compelled to remain, for you could not come back for me until you had finished."

" Oh! I do not fear that at all. I should not be afraid to stake my very existence that you will be much pleased; so much so, that you will not be in any hurry to get home again. All you have to do is, to say that you have made up your mind to go, and I will venture the rest myself."

" Very well; I will go. I can but try ; besides, I am anxious to pay a visit to the South ; I have heard so much about them, that really I have a great curiosity to see what kind of people they are."

" I dare say you will be as much pleased as I was."

" We shall see."

The conversation was interrupted by a rap at the door, which notified Mr. I—— that some one wished to see him.

Mrs. I—— had a very great prejudice of the South; she thought if she went there she should be among a set of barbarians at once. She was impressed with the idea that she should meet with a thousand such persons as Mrs. Stowe had conjured up in her imagination, in the shape of a man. But happily this was merely a freak of her own fancy, and we dare say that, if she had gone South, she would have been very agreeably disappointed.

Mrs. I—— was making great preparation for her visit South; for she thought, no doubt, that she should be looked upon as something wonderful; not dreaming for once that she should be amazed herself.

About a week after the conversation between herself and husband, they set off for their visit South. Mrs. I—— commenced to be charmed at once, as she got within the Southern States. Oh! how delightful and balmy was the air; how beautiful everything looked.

"What are all those fields in bloom? How beautiful are those delicate blossoms."

"That is a cotton field," replied Mr. I——; "you think it looks beautiful now, but when you see the white cotton bursting forth from the bud, you will think it still more lovely."

"What are all those little brown houses for? Listen to the music, and see how all the people are dancing; they seem to be very happy."

"That is a negro quarter, and those people you see dancing are slaves. Did I not tell you how happy they all seemed?"

"Well, really, they are very merry; just listen to the banjo! Oh! I see them plainer now; I see they are negroes. Are you sure they are slaves? They look too happy to be slaves."

"Yes, they are certainly slaves; and all those little houses you see are cabins. If you could just take a peep inside, you would be delighted. On a cold winter's evening they are seated around a large wood-fire, while others have large fires kindled out of doors, and dance around them."

"Well, really, I never could have believed that they would have seemed so happy."

"That is just what I tell you. Just wait until we arrive at Mr. M——'s plantation, you will be astonished still more."

"How long will it be before we get there?"

"I believe in a day or two. We have got through the greater part of our journey—that is, the staging."

"I am heartily glad of it, for I think nothing more disagreeable than riding in a stage on a dusty day, particularly when it is so excessively warm."

They had travelled but two days longer, when they came in sight of Mr. M——'s plantation.

"Look," exclaimed Mrs. I——, "what a number of cabins there are on that plantation. See, some of the slaves are sitting at the door, and others are smoking their pipes."

"I dare say they have just come in from their work, and are resting themselves. Whose place is this?"

"We are there at last—this is Mr. M——'s plantation. There is old Aunt Phebe now; just hear how she is singing. That is the way the slaves always do. That old man you see at the cabin door, smoking his pipe, is Uncle Dick."

"They all seem to be enjoying themselves, as though they were free."

"Certainly they do; why should they not? I am sure they have everything they desire, and I do not see why they should not be happy."

In a little while they drove up to the mansion of Mr. M——. Rufus ran to open the carriage-door, and greeted him with many bows and scrapes.

"How is yer, massa? Hopes I sees yer well. Dis ar' missus, what you fotch wid you? How is yer, missus?"

Mrs. I—— did not know what to make of all this politeness, and laughed heartily after Rufus left them.

In a few minutes Aunt Phebe received intelligence

that the 'litionist had come, and she said she would pretty soon show her what Phebe could do.

Mrs. M—— met Mrs. I—— with a very cordial welcome, and told her that she was extremely delighted to see her, and hoped that she would make herself at home.

"I had anticipated your arrival, consequently I prepared your room; it is a very pleasant part of the house, adjoining the veranda, and you will have a fine view of the country around. Everything is in bloom now, and there is a magnolia-tree fronting your window, and often a little bird sings there at night, called the 'southern nightingale.' I dare say you will be much pleased with it; just walk up and take a look at it. I dare say you are much fatigued from travelling, and feel very dusty; I will ring the bell for the servant to bring fresh water from our well; it has been pronounced excellent by all who have used it."

In a few minutes Laura appeared.

"I want you," said Mrs. M——, "to bring some water immediately for this lady. You are to be her waiting-maid, and must be very attentive to her."

After Laura left the room, Mrs. M—— told Mrs. I—— that Laura would be her maid so long as she stayed there, and that she was very trusty, indeed, and need not feel any hesitancy whatever in leaving any articles of jewelry on the dressing-table, for they would be perfectly safe.

"Well," said Mrs. I——, after Mrs. M—— left the room, "I do think Mrs. M—— is a lovely woman. How very amiable she is; I declare, no one could help loving her, she is so polite, and her manners are so winning. I am sure, if she continues this way, I shall love her very much. It is true enough what Mr. I—— said about the South; I do not think that I shall be in any particular hurry to get home."

In a few minutes Laura entered. As might be expected, she stared at Mrs. I——, for she had never before been in the company of a "Norrud lady."

"Shall I comb yer hair for yer, missus?" asked Laura, after she had viewed her well.

"No, I thank you; I can do it myself."

"I always combs missus', and I tought yer mought want me to comb yourn."

In a few minutes Laura was down on her knees.

"Missus, please, marm, put yer foot out a little furder, I can't git de string untied if yer don't."

"What do you want to untie the string for?"

"Why, bless my soul, I was gwine ter take yer shoes off. I habs dat ter do fer missus."

"I always take my shoes off myself, Laura."

"Well, well, if I eber seed de like; why, missus always calls me fer to do dat. You Norrud ladies don't do like de ladies Souf."

"No, Laura, we wait on ourselves. Ladies hadn't ought to wish to be waited on so much."

"Well, missus, what ar' de use of sarvents, den; ain't yer got any Norf?"

"O yes, but they are all white; but they do not work so hard as you slaves."

"Who do de work, den, missus?"

"We do the greater part of it ourselves."

"Cotch missus gwine in de kitchen. Aunt Phebe don't like ter hab folks boddering her, nohow; 'caze

she say dat de white folks don't know nuffin' 'bout de
kitchen, nohow. Well, missus, if I can't do nuffin' for
yer, I habs as well go, 'caze I 'spects missus wants
me."

Laura thought Mrs. I—— the strangest creature in
the world; and she went in full speed to Aunt Phebe's
cabin, to give an account of all that had passed.

"If eber I seed de 'like," said Laura; "I got down
on de floor to pull her shoes off for her, and she axed
me what I was doing down dar? Den when I told her,
she said, I do dat myself. Well, well; dat beats dis
nigger's time."

"Dat's jist like 'em," said Aunt Phebe; "I knowed
dat dem Norrud folks always do so. I 'spects we is
gwine to make 'em star' yit, afore dey go."

"She 'pears to be mighty 'ticular, 'deed. Missus put
me dar to wait on her, but I don't 'spects she will let
me do it."

Mr. I—— had been walking about the plantation
with Mr. M——, and now returned, as it was near tea
time.

"Well, how are you pleased, thus far," asked he of
his wife.

"Oh! I am delighted; how very affable Mrs. M——
is in her manners; I declare, any one would love her.
You would have laughed if you had been here a few
moments ago; there was a rich scene, indeed."

"Well, tell us what it was."

"Mrs. M——sent a servant to bring me water, and
told me that she was to be my waiting-maid. Well,

when she came in, she asked me if I wished her to comb my hair. I told her no, that I could do it myself."

"I expect the reason of it is this, she has been in the habit of dressing her mistress's hair."

"So she told me. She got down to take my shoes off, and seemed to think it very strange indeed, that I did not call on her to do it."

"You see the Southerners are very different from us; they have a great many servants, and they are waited on a great deal."

"But I should think it would make them indolent."

"O no; they are accustomed to it, you see, and that makes a great difference."

Rufus always waited on the table, and, wishing to look particularly nice, had fixed himself up, and thought that he looked exceedingly handsome.

When Mrs. I—— went in to tea, she noticed how smiling Rufus looked; and thought he must be very happy, or he would never have worn that countenance in the world.

Aunt Phebe had to go to the door, and take a peep through the keyhole, for she was extremely anxious to see the "Norrud lady;" besides, she had another object in view; she thought it very likely that she might hear some commendation passed upon her cakes. Sure enough, while Aunt Phebe was standing there, Mrs. I—— said—

"These cakes are very delightful, Mrs. M——, they are so very light; who made them? Really, I should like to get the receipt."

"My cook made them; her name is Phebe."

"The same one I told you about," said Mr. I—— to

16

his wife. "I noticed how delightful they were, the last time I was here."

"We have a first-rate cook," said Mr. M——, "and I would not give her in exchange for a dozen others."

Aunt Phebe heard all this, and could scarcely suppress her titter. She ran into the kitchen, to tell Uncle Dick about it.

"Didn't I say so, ole man? I told yer dat I would make dem star' wid my cakes. I'd like to see de one dat could beat Phebe; I know dey ain't any in dis country. You ought ter jist hab heerd 'em. How dey did talk; dey tought dey nebber had seen sich cakes in all dar life."

"I am mighty glad dat dey liked 'em, ole ooman; and I hopes dat yer will always meet wid sich good luck, and hab de bread and cake jist like it am to-night. Is dat yeast good what yer made de tother day?"

"I'se jist gwine to smell on it, for I want ter hab mighty nice family bread to-morrow morning for breakfast."

In a few days Mr. I—— left Mr. M——'s, to see about some business of importance.

"I leave my wife here, Mrs. M——, until I return."

"I shall be very happy to have you do so, and I will do all in my power to make her time pass off pleasantly."

"I have not the least doubt but what you will."

After Mr. I—— had gone, Mrs. M—— thought she would show Mrs. I—— about the plantation.

"I propose," said she to Mrs. I——, "to visit the cabins with you. I know what a prejudice you Northerners have to the Southerners, and I wish to show you the cabins of my slaves; then you can judge for yourself."

"Do you think they can be really happy?" asked Mrs. I——.

"I know it. They have all they desire, and I take great pleasure in doing all I can to promote their happiness. We will wait until this evening, when they all have finished their work, and get in their cabins. Then I will take you around. We have two free persons on the plantation; I have allowed them the privilege of retaining the cabin so long as they are pleased to stay. They were married a little while ago."

"Did they belong to you?"

"One of them did. The way of it was this: Benjamin (our slave) wished to marry a servant belonging to Mr. B——, on the adjoining plantation. He knew that her owners were going away soon, and that she would have to go too. So one day he went to Mr. M——, and related the whole circumstance to him. We then concluded to buy her, and set her free, and intended setting Ben free also. Her owners declined selling her; they gave her her freedom, and we did the same for Ben; and as they did not wish to leave this plantation, I gave them the liberty of remaining."

"You are very kind, indeed, Mrs. M——, for so doing."

"Oh! such things are very often done at the South. You all have a very mistaken idea about the Southerners, indeed. We treat our slaves as kindly as possible. I will show you all their cabins to-night."

Aunt Phebe heard that the "Norrud lady" would visit her cabin that night; so she went to work to have everything as nice as possible.

When night came, Mrs. M——, according to promise, took Mrs. I—— around to visit the cabins. The first was Aunt Phebe's. She was sitting down, smoking her pipe, mending the children's clothes. Uncle Dick was amusing Moses and Carey by telling them tales. Aunt Phebe seeing the lady coming, got up to welcome her.

"How does yer do, missus? I'se mighty glad ter see yer. Won't yer walk in?"

"No I thank you, Aunt Phebe," said her mistress; "I cannot come in now; I am only showing this lady around."

They visited each of the cabins; now but two remained—one was Rufus's and the other Ben's.

Ben sat there, playing on the banjo, while Lizzie was keeping step. "I tell yer what, Liz, yer can beat dem ar' folks what goes 'bout dancin', dat yer kin."

Lizzie seeing the ladies coming, stopped in a moment.

Mrs. M—— told Mrs. I—— that this was Ben, the banjo man. She desired him to play a tune or two, which he did very readily, and was very glad that his mistress had made the request of him. He was very anxious indeed to show off his extraordinary talent to the lady.

Mrs. I—— listened with delight and surprise, and then thanked him in a very polite manner.

In the adjoining cabin was Rufus, blacking up his boots, while Laura was starching his collar.

"I say, Rufus, I'se tired of starching dis collar; yer ain't got but dis white 'un, anyhow, and I tinks it is 'bout waring out; 'caze when I hold it up I can look through it. I heers somebody comin'. I wonder who it is?"

"Well, Rufus," said Mrs. M——, "how are you all coming on in here?"

"O berry well, missus, tank yer. How does yer all do?"

Mrs. M—— and her guest had heard the conversation about the collar, and enjoyed a hearty laugh before they entered the cabin.

"You all seem quite busy here."

"O yes, marm. You know dat we is gwine to hab a dance soon, and we is fixin' up for de 'casion."

"Well, good-night to you, Rufus and Laura; I hope you will get on well."

"Dat is dat 'Norrud lady,' I bets, what come round wid missus, to see dese cabins."

"Well, I wonder what she tought ob dis nigger; bery handsome, I knows."

All of the slaves had something to say about their visit, and each one wondered what was the opinion of Mrs. I—— respecting them.

"How were you pleased with the cabins, and the appearance of the slaves?" asked Mrs. M——.

"I was agreeably disappointed indeed. I had no idea that they were so happy. I thought they were afraid of their owners, and would not even dare to speak to them."

"I know that is exactly the idea you people North

have of the slaves South, and I know it is a very mistaken one."

"Are all other slaves like your own?"

"O yes; the greater part of them have good owners, and are treated very kindly indeed."

"I suppose it is not customary here to lash them, as I have often read of?"

"No, indeed; you must not give credit to all you read, written against the South. I cannot divine why the people of the North are so prejudiced against us. I know that we are slaveholders; but then we have all the trouble and expense of them; and besides, they are treated kindly."

Week after week passed. Mrs. I—— at last consented for Laura to wait upon her, and learned from her the condition of the slaves.

Mrs. I—— had received several letters from her husband, and when she answered them she did not express any desire whatever of going home, she had become so completely infatuated with the South. She had become quite a Southerner, too, since her arrival there, and began to think she should like to make a longer visit than she at first anticipated.

"Laura, Laura, do come here and take off my shoes; really, I am too much fatigued to do it myself. Then hand me a glass of water."

From this Laura went to obey the commands of the "Norrud lady," and began to think she liked to be waited on as well as any one else did.

"Well, well," said Laura, "if I eber seed de like ob dat. Yer ought jist ter hab seen her, Aunt Phebe;

dar she was, callin' for water, and den she wanted me to pull off her shoes, and dress her hair.''

"I tole yer so—I knowed it; 'caze when dese Norrud folks come Souf, dey don't care 'bout being waited on; but jist wait awhile, and I bets you hears 'em callin' on fer dese niggers.''

Mrs. I—— had, in fact, become quite an advocate for being waited on, and she took good care to call Laura upon every occasion.

"I'se really tired ob waitin' on dat lady what comed from de Norf; when she fust come here den she want me to do nuffin', and now, bless my soul, I 'specks to war all my shoes out walking arter her.''

Mrs. I—— had been there about two months, when her husband arrived. She had not become at all weary of her visit; she began to think that the South was a charming place, and would like to live there.

" Are you most ready to go home?" asked Mr. I——.

" I am not particularly anxious to go; but, if business calls you home, I will get ready to go, although I would like to stay a longer time.''

" How have you passed your time?''

" I never enjoyed myself more in all my life; and I am determined, from this time forward, to eradicate everything like prejudice for the South. I never, in all my life, enjoyed myself more.''

"Tell me what you think of the treatment of the slaves.''

" I do honestly say, I believe they are far better off than our white servants North. They are not cruelly treated; it is quite the contrary.''

"I am glad you have so good an opinion of the South, and I hope you will inform your friends how mistaken they are in regard to the South, and the treatment of the slaves."

"That I will most certainly do. But I know it will be a hard matter to convince them of the fact; for I know how incredulous I was until I saw for myself. . Dear me! I do not know what I shall do when I go home, for then I shall have to wait on myself. I do wish I had such a servant as Laura."

"You found her very polite and obliging, then?"

"Yes, indeed; she could not have been more so. When shall we leave?"

"In a very short time; perhaps in a week, or less time than that; it depends upon the letter I get. I expect one to-morrow that will decide positively for us."

To-morrow came, and, much to the chagrin of Mrs. I——, she was to leave in less time than a week. She really felt sad, for she had become so much attached to Mrs. M——, that she felt as though she were parting from her dearest friend. But we are doomed to leave those we love the most. From this time, Mrs. I—— ever held up for the South, and often spoke of what fell under her observation while she was there; and nothing could offend her more than to hear any one speaking against the South.

CHAPTER XVII.

MRS. I——'S RETURN HOME—A CONVERSATION AMONG
VISITORS.

"HAVE you heard of Mrs. I——'s arrival? You know she has been South for some time?"

"No; when did she come?"

"About a week ago, I think. I am going to see her this morning, and hear what she has to say about the South."

"I have a notion to go, too."

"Well, do go. I dare say she will be much pleased to see us all."

"I am very much surprised, indeed, that she should have stayed there so long. I once heard her say she would not go among those slave-holders for anything. You may depend upon it, she has had some inducement."

These remarks passed between some friends of Mrs. I——. They had heard of her visit to the South, and were very anxious, indeed, to hear what she had to say; so they all went to call on Mrs. I——.

"We have come to congratulate you on your safe arrival. How were you pleased with your trip South?"

"I could not possibly give you any idea of my visit. I never was so charmed with a place in all my life. I declare, I never saw so much hospitality in all my life. You really do not know what Southern life is."

"Nor do I wish to know," replied one of the visitors.

"That is just what I thought myself once," replied Mrs. I.——. "I know when Mr. I—— first came home, and spoke in such glowing terms of the South, I would not listen to a word of it. At last he prevailed on me to go South with him; I certainly do not regret having gone, and would like to go again."

"I am very much surprised to hear you talk so, Mrs. I——; how could you endure staying there among those slave-holders?"

"Why, there are no better people to be found in the world than Southerners."

"How in the world can you call those set of torturers good?"

"I am not going to hear one word said against the Southerners, for I was treated so kindly there; and, as to being a set of torturers, they are quite the reverse."

"Oh! you need not tell me that; I have heard enough about them."

"So you may; but it is all false, I tell you."

"So you have turned Southerner in notions?"

"O no, not by any means; only so far as I know they are correct."

"Then you think slave-holding all very proper?"

"I said nothing about slave-holding. I know one thing very well—they are treated as kindly as they could be, and are happy enough, far happier than any of our white servants; for they have kind owners, who care for them, and will do anything to make them comfortable."

"You talk about a slave knowing what comfort is!"

"If they do not know what comfort is, I am sure I do not. I just wish you could have seen as much of them as I did; they all live as happily as they possibly can."

"How those Southerners have made you believe things."

"I saw for myself; they did not endeavor to influence me in the least."

"You might not have thought so, but they have a way of getting around people."

"I do not believe a Southerner would do that!"

"I see that it is of no use arguing with you any longer; and you are so completely infatuated with the South, that I should not be very much surprised if you were to make up your mind to go there for good."

"It is certainly a very delightful climate to live in. It is like a perfect Indian-summer through the whole winter, I am told. I think I should like to spend one there."

"What do you think of the manners of the Southerners?"

"I never met with more affability of manners in my life. The lady with whom I stayed was certainly very winning and attractive. She was so courteous; it did seem to me that she could not do enough for her guests. She took me all around, one evening, to visit the cabins, after the slaves had all come in from their work, and it really made my heart glad to see them. Every Saturday night they have a great time among themselves; sometimes they sing and dance. They have their own peculiar way of dancing, and they seem to enter into the spirit of it too."

"I suppose they have to labor very hard, poor creatures!"

"No, they are not compelled to work half so hard as our common laborers; they are not so exposed to the weather, either. I suppose they have to work, of course, but then their owners do not exact too much from them."

"Do you not think they must feel very unhappy when they reflect that they are slaves?"

"I do not believe they ever give it a thought, for they are much more free than our servants."

"I cannot think a slave can be happy, for they know that they are doomed to bondage all their lives; they know, very well, there is no chance of their being free."

"You are much mistaken there, for I know of a slave who was set free by his owners. It was on the very same plantation, too, where I visited in the summer. They sometimes refuse their freedom, because they are afraid that their owners will not allow them to stay with them after they are free."

"Strange slaves they must be, not to wish their freedom."

"You see, they know they are better off as they are, than to be thrown on their own resources. Pray, tell me, what would they have to depend upon?"

"Why, they could go to work!"

"They might have to work much harder than they do now. Besides, their pay is apt to be small, hardly enough for them to subsist upon. Do not tell me about those free negroes, they are not half so well taken care

of by themselves as their owners take care of them before they had their freedom."

"I never thought you would entertain the opinion
you do about slaves."

"It is not very probable that I ever should if I had
not seen and know what I do."

The visitors had made quite a long stay; the fact was,
they were so much taken up with the subject on which
they were conversing that they did not regard the time
at all.

"Did you know, Mrs. A——, that we have been here
too hours at least?"

"No, indeed, you certainly must be mistaken!"

"Just look at your watch, then, and see for yourself."

"Dear me, so we have; well, really, I must go!"

In a little while they separated, thinking that Mrs.
I—— entertained very peculiar notions, and wondered
how she could think as she did.

"I had three visitors this morning," said Mrs. I——
to her husband, as they sat down to dinner.

"Who were they?"

"Mrs. A——, and two other ladies."

"What did they have to say?"

"Oh! they got pretty warm on the subject of slavery,
and they think that I have turned quite a Southerner
in notions; they seemed very much surprised that I
should hold up for the South; but I just told them
plainly that all my prejudices regarding the South had
vanished; that I had seen enough to convince me that

17

I was in error. I do not like to hear any one speaking against the South."

"Do you not remember when I first came home, how incredulous you were? I could not convince you that you were in error then."

"But my opinion has changed since that time. I never should have thought so much of the South if I had not visited there. I only wish our own people possessed some of their hospitality; I know that it would make them render each other more happy. Is there not all the difference in the world in them?"

"Certainly, the difference is very perceptible, indeed. Well, tell me what conclusion you all arrived at this morning?"

"They said it was no use to argue with me any longer, that the Southerners had stuffed me up with their notions, and they were very much surprised to see me governed by them."

"Then there was no convincing them?"

"None in the world."

"Well, you must make all allowances for them; remember your own case at one time, and that will serve to make you more lenient towards others."

"But it is so provoking to hear them talk in that way about slaves and slave-holders. I have no patience with them, at all."

"I know how provoking it is to be differed with; but you must expect that. Remember there is a great diversity of opinion in the world; all people do not think alike, and, besides, every one thinks his own way the best."

"But I like to have people listen to reason."

"Oh! you know, when anything concerning slavery comes up, they will not hear of its being sanctioned."

"I know that; but they ought not to contradict. I really believe they differ for perversion sake."

"O no, I guess not. Did you differ from that cause, when I was talking to you when I first returned from the South?"

"No, indeed; I really thought you wrong then."

"Well, that is just exactly the case with your friends who called here this morning. Nothing will ever convince them to the contrary, without witnessing what you did; and I am sure you would not have done so either."

Mrs. I—— began to be a little more considerate after a while, yet she should not hear a word against the South without feeling offended.

So much for Southern hospitality; and, if we would follow their example, there would be more harmony in the world. Every one should treat a stranger kindly, whoever he may be. Ofttimes a simple word or kind act is remembered through life, and may serve to gain us a friend when we most need one.

CHAPTER XVIII.

THE PARTING.

" This is the last day we shall be together, dear Lydia, in these classic halls. Oh! how my heart sighs to think I so soon must leave one whom I so dearly love. We part, and know not what time death may call us away from earth; we may not behold the face of each other again; no more, perhaps, will that sunny smile of yours beam upon me. I look around now, and behold all nature clad in beauty; I hear the little birds, as they chant their themes; I listen to the zephyrs, as they whisper through the green foliage, and they seem to sigh for me. Oh! would that I could always be with you. Many, yes, many happy hours have we passed together; and, when I reflect upon them, they will cause me to feel the deepest anguish. Truly has one said that ' our greatest pleasures cause us the greatest pain.' I, who have been with you four years, shared your love and confidence, must leave you. If I had not participated in that enjoyment, then I should have no cause for so much regret. As strangers we met, but soon a friendship sprang up between us, and it will ever continue to exist. I love you too fondly, ever to change; you, dear Lydia, are among the dearest objects of my heart. I would not say ' farewell' to you so soon; no, no; gladly would I longer share your sweet society, for I feel that none love me more, or would be more true to me, than yourself. All I ask is, that you will sometimes remember me.

"Will you not sometimes, too, cast a thought on Dora? Remember she will be unchanged, however much things may alter. Will you not love me as in days gone by? Ofttimes the thoughts of days spent in these halls will cross your memory, and you will hear in imagination the echo of those merry peals of laughter which so oft have resounded through these halls. Amid all these recollections, think of Dora. I will not say 'adieu' to you, dear Lydia; I can better write it. I cannot say 'farewell' to one whom I so fondly love. I but ask that you will not forget your attached Dora."

The examination had closed; the girls were all preparing to leave the next morning. Lydia had been sent for by Mrs. P——, and, during her absence, Dora wrote this little note, and placed it upon the table. She felt that she could express her feelings better in writing, for she knew her heart would become too full to tell Lydia what she so much wished. Reader, have you ever parted with a much-loved friend, one whom you felt was the dearest object of your heart? Have you spent many happy hours in her society, and felt as though nothing on earth could give you more pleasure than to be with that friend? Have you then been doomed to part with her? If so, then you can fully appreciate the feelings of Dora. She sat down to write the note just as the sun was setting. She was near an open window; and, as she watched the fading beams as they receded from view, she felt that ere it would set again she would be far away from her dear Lydia. As she traced the lines, tears fell upon the paper, for heavy was her heart. Just as she had sealed the note, and put it upon the table, Lydia appeared.

"Have you been here ever since Mrs. P—— sent for me?" asked Lydia.

"Yes, I have been sitting by the window ever since you left the room."

"What have you been doing with yourself? I see that your eyes look as though you had been crying; it reminds me of the cloud upon the sun."

Dora's tears started afresh. Oh! no one knew the burden which was resting upon her heart.

"My dear friend, it makes me feel very unhappy to see you looking so sad. If I could dry your tears, I would gladly do it with all my heart. I dare say I know the cause of your grief; but we must part. But be cheered with the hope that soon we shall see each other again; do not allow yourself to give way to your feelings."

"Lydia, I cannot refrain from weeping. You know that we are doomed to part, and I shall have to remain here another whole term without you. I do not believe I can stay; I will write to father to let me come home, and I know that he will grant my request when he sees how very unhappy I am."

"I am quite sure that he would let you come home, but you must not think of any such thing, I beg of you. Your education is of more importance to you than you may be aware of. I should feel very badly if I thought you would not remain here another term. Only think, you will be in the senior class, and the time will not appear

very long to you. Will you not promise me that you
will stay ? Try to overcome all these feelings, and I
know you will never regret having remained."

"If you were going to be here, I should not feel any
hesitancy whatever; but I cannot bear the thoughts of
being here when you are away. Everything will remind
me of you ; the school-room, the class-room, the play-
grounds ; yes, everything !"

" Just determine that you will stay, my dear friend,
and I feel that in after years you will be glad for having done so."

" Well, for your sake, Lydia, I promise ; nothing
gives me greater pleasure than pleasing you."

Dora, wishing to give Lydia an opportunity of reading the note, made an excuse to leave the room, going
to the table at the same time under the pretence of getting a book.

Lydia saw something like an envelope, and took it
up. Dora hastily left the room. Lydia was a little
surprised on looking at the direction to find that it was
to herself.

" That is just what Dora has been doing up here all
this time. She is a dear creature, and it distresses
me to know that she is so unhappy, and it is all because
she loves me so much. I would not for the world have
her cease loving me ; but I should feel much better contented if she would endeavor to subdue her feelings.
But I must hasten to read the note."

" ' Oh ! would I could always be with you.' Only
see what depths of feeling she has; how much do these
words of affection contain. They come from a faithful
and confiding heart ; such language could never have

eminated from any other source than that of a true and
loving heart."

Lydia mused much upon the note; often she had
read it, and heartily wished that she could assuage the
grief of Dora.

"I will answer it," said she to herself, "or else she
may think I care nothing for her. I would not give
one pang to her tender heart for all earth affords. It
is near twilight, but I can see to write to her a few lines,
enough at least to show her that I highly appreciate
her note; yes, every word here traced. Oh! that all
could boast of such a heart of innocency as she pos-
sesses, how happy would all be!"

Lydia seated herself to reply to the note, and determined to place it in her hand the morning they parted;
the note ran as follows:—

"It is twilight's hour, dear Dora; a meet one, indeed, to hold
communion with such a spirit as thine. The zephyrs are now
sporting amid the leaves of the trees which shade my window,
and seem to say 'be happy, be gay.' Then wilt thou not endeavor to be gay, if it is only for the sake of one in whose every
thought you dwell? I would not see thy sunny brow shaded with
grief; oh, no, wear that same sweet smile ever. Be as gay as
when we met; hope that our parting will be but for a brief time.
Thou knowest not, dear Dora, what happy changes time may
bring for us both, my darling friend. I trust that life may ever
be bright before thee. Gladly would I stay with thee if it consti-
tutes thy happiness in the least; but I cannot follow my wishes,
for circumstances will not permit. I ask but one simple request
of thee, and that is, try to be happy; let not the thoughts of my
being absent disturb thee; for although we may be many miles
apart, yet will I ever be near thee in spirit, and hold commune
with thy own dear self. Light is fast fading, and I can scarcely
see how to trace these lines.

" Adieu to thee, Dora, dear ; I trust that ere long we shall be together again. That such may be the case is the heartfelt wish of   " Your attached
" LYDIA."

It was generally the custom with the school-girls to have a dance on the evening the examination closed. They all participated in the amusement, and seemed to be very happy. The thoughts of going home and meeting kind friends made their youthful hearts throb with joy.

Among them all, Lydia and Dora were the only ones absent. Instead of dancing, they had gone off together to have a little talk, as the time they had to remain in each other's society was fast drawing to a close.

It was a lovely moonlight night, the stars were smiling upon them as they sat in the arbor, talking.

"I was thinking, Lydia," said Dora, "how sad I shall feel whenever I come to this arbor after you have left. I shall love to come, for it will remind me of yourself; yet I know it will cause me to have many sad thoughts."

" You must think of me, Dora, my sweet friend, whenever you come here ; remember that my spirit will be near you, although we may be many miles apart. Does not everything appear very sad to-night ?"

" Yes, my dear friend, and it is but the sympathy of our own hearts. I was observing how lovely everything appeared, but I dare say it is ourselves, for we feel so sadly that we are apt to imagine that everything else looks and feels the same."

"I wish I could dispel the gloom which broods

over my own heart; I am sure I would gladly do it for
your own sake, dear Lydia."

"Then do endeavor to chase it away. I am sure
that nothing could render me more happy."

"We will retire now, and slumber will bury in obli-
vion, for a while, at least, all our grief."

"Oh! would that it could make me forget always;
but too soon I shall awaken again to the sad reality of
parting with you. I shall have to remain here all this
vacation, excepting the time I am at the examination
of my brother."

"You can write to me, and advise me of what you
are doing."

"Yes, and if you will promise to be prompt in reply-
ing, I will content myself."

"We had better not remain out here any longer, for
the night air is very cool. I shall always keep in re-
membrance this evening."

"So shall I, dear Lydia, and it will make me feel
very sad whenever I visit this spot again; you, dearest,
will be associated with it always."

The morning came, bright and beautiful. Never did
the hills look more lovely in their emerald garment;
here and there a little blue-eyed violet peeped up
above the tall grass, like a fairy spirit, clad in robes
of blue.

Dora awakened, and her first thoughts were of the
parting. She endeavored to be happy, but could not.

Lydia was packing her trunk; Dora looked towards
her, and her eyes filled with tears.

After they had completed their toilet, they went out

to take a last peep at the play-grounds. They happened to look down the hill, and behold, who should Lydia see but her brother, coming towards them.

"There is Harry; I am going to meet him."

In a few minutes they met; it had been a long time since she had seen him.

"It is near time for the cars to come by, and you had better be in readiness. By the by, where is your friend Dora?"

"I will go and call her; you can entertain her until I return."

We will leave Dora and Harry conversing, while we notice the parting of Lydia with the teachers and principal. The first person to whom she bid adieu was Mrs. P——.

"You are going to leave us to-day, Lydia. I regret much to part with you. I give you much credit for your progress in your studies, and the attention which you have paid to them. Your deportment has always been such as never to deserve any censure whatever; you will be missed, both by the instructors and pupils. I hope, Lydia, that your pathway in life may be ever bright, and that all the expectations of your anxious parents may be realized. As a scholar, you have been very exemplary, and all the teachers accord with me in giving you commendation for your deportment. I shall ever think of you, and have that high regard for you that I now have. I bid you adieu, Lydia, with great reluctance, and heartily wish that all the young ladies under my charge had the same dignity of character, and paid that attention to their studies that you have done."

Lydia's time was limited; so she bid adieu to Mrs. P——, and went in quest of the other instructors, who expressed the same sentiments as Mrs. P——.

With a sorrowful heart she gave one more look to the loved mansion and its inmates, and then went to the arbor, where she found Dora and her brother awaiting her. The saddest of all was to come yet—the most bitter tears were to be shed. She scarcely knew how to say farewell to Dora. "But it must be," thought Lydia; and after many loving looks, and exchange of sentiment—Dora and Lydia, the two dear friends, parted.

Reader, if you would know the pangs then felt, think of a mother who has just lost an only and much loved child; then you can judge of their feelings.

CHAPTER XIX.

CHARLES AGAIN—GRADUATES—RECEIVES THE VALEDICTORY ADDRESS.

SINCE the difficulty about the fishing-pond, Charles had become more cautious than ever. He was particularly attentive to the regulations of the college, more so than he had been in time past. The instructors regarded him with pleasure, and often spoke of his untiring assiduity, and even feared lest it might injure his health. Five years had elapsed since he first came to the college, and he was now about finishing his course of study. He looked back upon the time when he thought how long it would be before he graduated, and now saw how rapidly it had fled.

He had not been home once during that long, long time ; and when he reflected that he should soon be home again, his heart swelled with joy. "Oh!" thought he, " I shall so soon see my own home ; it has been quite a period since I left it, and what a hearty welcome I shall meet with. There will be old Uncle Dick ; I expect his head is frosted, by this time ; his step is more feeble than ever, and his eyesight more dim. How delighted he will be to see me. I know I have changed very much, for when I came here I was but a mere boy. Uncle Dick will have to look up to me now, instead of

18

down. I care not how soon the time comes for me to go home, for I wish to see them all."

These were the thoughts which passed through the mind of Charles the day before the "commencement." He had been honored by having the valedictory address to write. The instructors convened some time before the examination was to take place, for the purpose of deciding who should have the honor, and they unanimously agreed upon Charles M——. " He has," said they, " been all a student could possibly be; his studies are always perfect; when he comes to the class-room his conduct is exemplary, and his regard for the instructors is unequalled by any in the college."

The President also agreed that Charles M—— should write the valedictory address. Of course, among the students, there was quite a dissension, as might be expected; but, had they allowed themselves to consider for a moment, they would have agreed with the Faculty in saying Charles deserved the honor conferred.

So soon as Charles was apprised of the fact, he went right to work to write it. He studied the theme well, and it gained the applause of all who heard it.

Commencement day came. The hall was crowded with a concourse of people; all came with ears and eyes open.

Essay after essay was read, until, at last, Mr. Charles M—— was called upon to read the valedictory address. All listen attentively, and are astonished with the masterly piece of composition; his eloquence, his gesture, attracted the attention of all; even their admiration was excited.

The house rang with applauses, and all the professors looked on with feelings of gratification. In the mean time one of the professors went out with one of the students and twined a wreath of laurel; so soon as Charles descended the stage, they presented it to him.

Mr. and Mrs. M—— felt almost an ecstasy when they saw what a splendid examination he passed. They knew that their expense and pains had not been squandered upon him, and hoped he would adorn the society in which he mingled.

Dora caught every word which fell from his lips, and it gave a new impetus to her desire to pursue her studies. She fully determined in her own mind to do herself as much credit at her examination, for she knew what satisfaction it would afford her parents. When she saw the President of the college presenting her brother with a wreath, she could have wept with joy, and hoped she might be deserying of such an honor on the day of her graduation.

After the close of the examination, Mr. and Mrs. M—— lavished many commendations upon their son, and at the same time told Dora to follow the example of her brother.

"I will see what I can show you all twelve months hence," said Dora; "and I sincerely hope that all my expectations will be realized."

The students, the professors, and the audience flocked around Charles to compliment him upon his success, and expressed a desire that he might meet with the same all through life.

Oh! what a pleasure it must have been to a devoted

parent, who has expended so much upon the education of a child, to see their efforts thus crowned with success ; and what a joy too it must have caused the heart of that child, that he had made good use of the time.

Many presents were given Charles by the different members of the Faculty, as a token of the high regard they entertained for him. When he left the college, all felt a reluctance in bidding him adieu, and gave him a pressing invitation to visit them, and keep them in knowledge of all his undertakings.

Charles felt indeed that he left many true friends ; those, too, who were interested in his welfare in life, and who had taught "the young idea how to shoot." He thought upon the past with pleasure, for he felt that he had conducted himself properly, and won the approbation of all the teachers. He told them that he should always look back upon the past with pleasure, and number the days spent in those classic halls among the happiest of his life.

Contrary to the expectations of Dora, she did not have to remain at school any part of the vacation ; for from L—— they went on a tour to some watering-place, and passed the summer very pleasantly indeed ; and by the time they had completed their jaunt, it was time for Dora to return again to school.

Charles saw that Dora felt sad about going back ; he knew very well that Lydia had left, and having a very sympathizing heart, he talked to her upon the subject.

"I see, sister, that you feel badly about returning to school. I am heartily sorry to know that you are so sad. Do not give up to your feelings ; reflect upon the work before you; it is of vast importance, and I do assure you that you will never regret in after life that you returned. Press on, and you may be crowned with honors. Always act in such a way as to secure the esteem of all the teachers; attend to your studies attentively, and I know that you will not regret having done so. I know that you will feel lonely without your friend, but endeavor to forget all for the present, and think only of your studies. I know, by so doing, time will hang less heavily with you. The senior year is one of trial; you know you are, as it were, summing up all your studies, and preparing for your final examination. Go, then, sister, with a light heart to your studies, and do your best, and I know that success will crown you."

Dora felt the force of her brother's remarks, and thought of the honors of the examination. So she just made up her mind to do as he said.

In a few days, Dora found herself at R—— again. All the girls met her with a hearty welcome, particularly those of the senior class, who hailed her as one of their sister classmates.

We will now leave Dora for awhile, and accompany Charles home, and see with what reception he met.

Charles thought that a journey certainly had never seemed so long to him before. He was anxious to get home, consequently his parents stopped as little on the way as possible. As they went along, how familiar everything looked to Charles, although a very long time had elapsed since he last travelled that way.

One evening, Uncle Dick was seated at his cabin-door (about two weeks after Charles started for home), smoking his pipe. He did not expect them so soon. He was regaling himself nicely, when all at once he heard a carriage coming.

"Ole ooman, I hears a carriage comin'. I wonders who's in dar?"

"I 'specks it's massa."

"No, 'tain't; 'caze 'tain't time for him to come yit."

Uncle Dick watched until the carriage drove up. Charles was the first one to get out.

"Dat ar' gemman ain't Massa Charles, nohow, 'caze he ain't tall like dat."

"I bets it is," said Aunt Phebe; "for he mought growed since den. I'se gwine to see, anyhow."

"Do go, ole ooman, for de rumatiz has crippled me so dat I can't walk fast, nohow."

Aunt Phebe went, sure enough; and, after a while, she exclaimed, "Massa Charles, Massa Charles! why you is growed so big, and so purty, too. I neber 'spected dat I would see you 'gin; but now I sees you standin' right afore my face."

Uncle Dick hearing her, went as fast as his feeble limbs would permit, and in a little while was almost down upon his knees.

"Oh! how glad I is to see yer, Massa Charles. Yer is so big, and den so purty, jist as ole ooman said. Massa Charles, does yer hab any recollection ob dat kite what yer left here when you went 'way?"

"O yes, Uncle Dick. But you have not kept it all this time, have you?"

"Ain't I? I'se got it now; an', if yer will jist wait till de mornin', I will show yer if I ain't got it."

"You don't think that I will ever use it again, do you, Uncle Dick?"

"O no, massa, I 'specks not; but I kin jist show you, an' you kin see how nice I has kept it."

"Oh! certainly; and I will look at it with a great deal of pleasure."

In a little while, Rufus, Ben, and all the rest of the slaves, came in to welcome their Master Charles. They all thought he had grown very much, and said they should never have known him. Uncle Dick thought he never felt so happy before in all his life. He said, "Massa Charles come now; he berry glad, 'caze he will hab somebody to talk to him now."

There was quite a commotion on the plantation that night; they could talk of nothing else but the arrival of their young master. Aunt Phebe said that she wished Miss Dora would come, too, for she wanted to see her, and hoped that it would not be long before she came back to the South.

"Well," said Rufus, "what shall we all hab to 'muse Massa Charles? I say, ole Snubs (speaking to Ben), s'pose we all has a dance; an', if yer will jist tune up dat ar' banjo, dis nigger will hab his boots blacked up, an' de collar starched stiff, and den we will all hab a merry time. What says yer?"

"I 'grees to dat; an' if yer will jist go round an' tell all dem ar' darkies, I tink we kin git it up. Yer knows it has been a mighty long time since we danced any afore young massa, an' I 'specks he will like it mighty well."

"Yes," said Aunt Phebe, "I wish yer young folks would hab one; but den I don't want yer to make yerself a fool, Rufus, 'caze yer knows dat yer wants to show off, anyhow."

"Neber mind me for dat, 'caze I kin 'have myself any time."

"Well, I hopes yer will do it, den."

A new thought struck Rufus—he had an idea of serenading his master that night; so he tells Ben about it, who, of course, agrees. The banjo is then tuned up in nice order for the occasion. Every slave seemed so anxious to do something to prove to Charles that he had met with a hearty welcome.

Being very much fatigued, he retired early; about twelve o'clock, he was awakened by the music of the banjo and singing. He thought it sounded very pleasantly at that late hour of the night. The moon was shining, and he looked out from his window to see who the musicians were.

There stood Ben with the banjo, and Moses with the tambourine, to join the chorus; there was Rufus and several others besides. They sang "Hither we come," "Come ye darkies all."

Charles was very much amused and delighted with the serenade, and could not refrain from smiling to see them in such high glee.

Aunt Phebe and Uncle Dick could not make up the party, for they were too old and infirm, but their will was good.

Charles visited all the cabins the next day, and he saw very little change. He looked at the one Aunt Nelly used to occupy, and it brought to memory her death and that of little Hannah. The two favorite dogs,

Punch and Judy, ran out to welcome him; although he had been gone so long, yet they had not forgotten him.

As Charles looked around and saw everything appearing so natural as in days gone by, he had peculiar feelings pass over him.

"How long a time," thought he, "has elapsed since I left home. Providence has blessed me with kind parents, and every comfort of life. What delight it gives me to know that all the slaves are so contented and happy here. I know they could not be better off if they were free. I have been North, and I know the state of the servants there; I have compared them to the slaves South, and, were I in their places, I would rather be a slave on this plantation than to be a white servant at the North."

He went to Aunt Phebe's cabin, and there found Uncle Dick smoking his pipe. As soon as he saw him, he was up in a minute.

"Come in, massa, come in; I'se mighty glad to see yer. When yer left me, den, yer was nuffin' but a chile; but jist see here, ole ooman, what a fine large gemman he is. Do tell us, massa, 'bout de Norf, how does yer like it?"

"Oh! very much indeed, Uncle Dick, but you know I prefer the South; the people are more warm-hearted here."

"Yes, dat dey is, dat dey is; does yer tink dat de sarvants dar is well off as we is?"

"Well, no, Uncle Dick! I don't think they are. I believe you would like the South anyhow."

"Dat I would. Catch dis nigger eber going dar 'mong dem 'litionists. Wait a minute, massa, I wants ter show yer dat kite what I put 'way when yer went ter de Norf."

The kite was brought forward; it was as good as ever, save some few holes the rats had made.

"Yer see, massa, de rattons knawed dis, and hang 'em, I will kill 'em if I cotched dem at it."

"Well, Uncle Dick, I think you have taken very good care of my kite, and we will keep it just for the sake of old times."

"So we will. Here, Mose, put it back; be kefful!"

Charles remained some time talking to Uncle Dick, and answered many questions of Aunt Phebe, concerning Dora. She was much delighted at the idea of seeing her soon, and said she hoped she would live to see that time.

Rufus came to Charles and told him that two gentlemen were awaiting him in the parlor; so he left Uncle Dick, promising to come to see him again soon.

Uncle Dick now resumes his pipe, and reflects upon the days gone by when he used to help his young Master Charlie to fly his kite, and sighed that they had passed, no more to return.

CHAPTER XX.

PLANTATION DANCE.

THE slaves were making great preparations for the dance, which they intended giving in honor of the arrival of their young master. Ben had practised over some of his favorite reels, and Moses accompanied him with the tambourine. Rufus had his boots and collar fixed up, of course. While Laura and Lizzie were making preparations for their toilet.

Aunt Phebe and Uncle Dick said, as it was a warm dry night, they would just go out and look at them.

A supper was to be prepared for them, to which Mrs. M—— had largely provided; and they concluded that the table should be set in front of Aunt Phebe's cabin.

The dancers were to arrange themselves near the back porch of Mrs. M——'s mansion; and Charles, together with Mrs. and Mr. M——, were to be the spectators.

The morning prior to the great dance, Ben met his master, and, of course, made known the proposition to him.

"I say, Massa Charles, I'se mighty glad to see yer."

"I am the same, I assure you, Rufus !"

"Well, massa, we niggers was tinking 'bout habin' a dance, and missus say how she got no 'jections to it. What say yer to it, massa ?"

"I shall be very much pleased, indeed, to see you all dancing. It has been a very long time since I have seen a plantation dance. I often used to think of them when I was at the North. I never saw so much merriment among the white slaves there as I do here. You ought to be very happy, Ben; for I tell you that you are well off, better off than you think for."

"I knowed dat fust, massa; I heerd tell ob Norrud folks afore dis time, an' I bet you wouldn't catch dis nigger libing 'mong 'em. Tell me 'bout dem folks dar, dey know nuffin' 'bout dese times we see down here. Wonders if dey eber hab a plantation dance?"

"No, Ben, I never saw anything of the sort there. You know at the North they have no cotton plantations like they do South."

"How does dey git de cotton, den?"

"We furnish them with it. That is the reason why father has it done up in bales, to send away."

"What does dey do wid so much?"

"They put it to different uses; clothing is made of it, and various other things. They have large factories at the North for that purpose; they are called cotton factories, and a great many persons are employed in them. I would much rather be in your place, Ben, than of a person who works in those factories; for they have to work very hard, indeed, and it is so very laborious, too."

"I knows all dat; massa tell me 'bout dem. I know dat you ain't gwine to cotch me down dar, nohow. Do dey hab any 'litionists dar where you war."

At first Charles did not understand him exactly, but

in a moment it occurred to him that Ben meant abolitionists.

"O yes, Ben, we have a plenty of them. I never saw a slave the whole time I was there; you know they are all free at the North, or else the servants are white."

"Did dey talk to yer 'bout de darkies down Souf?"

"O yes, Ben; but I made it a rule, before I went there, not to enter into any controversy with them at all; so I did not speak to them very often on the subject of slavery."

"Dat's right, massa; neber quarrel wid nobody, 'caze it ain't right, nohow."

It seems that Ben had got pretty far from the track. He had come for the purpose of asking his master about the dance, and he had got upon quite another subject altogether.

"So, massa, yer say dat yer would likes to hab us dance for yer. You must sot out on de back porch, an' we is all gwine to dance afore it, so dat you, missus, and massa kin see us. You know dat de moon rises mighty soon now o' nights, so you kin see us all."

"Who plays the banjo, Ben? I believe you do, of course."

"Yes, yes, massa, dat I does. I like to see anybody dat kin beat dis nigger doin' dat."

Charles could not refrain from smiling, to hear Ben thus commending himself.

"I'se gwine now, massa, to 'form de niggers dat we will hab de great dance to-night, an' to tell 'em dat dey must do dar best. So you'll 'scuse me now, massa."

"Certainly, Ben. I wish you much success to-night."

19

" Tank yer, sar."

Rufus was the first one who received the information, and, as might be expected, was much elated. He thought how he would show off that night, and he could think of nothing else all that day but the plantation dance.

At sunset they all came in from their work. Charles was sitting on the porch, looking at them as they passed. Some were singing, others were laughing and talking; they all seemed to be in great glee. Charles could but compare them with the white slaves at the North. " At sunset," thought he, " the slaves all come in from their work, and go to their little cabins and enjoy themselves, while the white servants at the North have no such comfort; it is entirely unknown to them."

Charles had had an opportunity of comparing them, for he had been North five years; and he was forcibly struck with the difference between his own slaves and the white servants at the North.

Old Uncle Dick took his pipe, and seated himself at his cabin door; he had become much more decrepit and infirm since Charles left home. He did not do any work now, but merely went into the cotton-fields to show the younger ones how to do.

Charles, seeing him, thought he would go and talk to him a little while.

" Bless yer soul, massa, how does yer do to-day ? I ain't seed you afore, to-day."

" No, I don't think you have ; I have not seen you, either. I hear you all are going to have a great time to-night."

" So it 'pears, massa."

"I suppose you do not intend to join it, do you, Uncle Dick?"

"Me jine in it, massa? No, sar; de rumatiz tuck me some time ago, an' I ain't walked good since. If I was to go to dancin', I 'speck dem niggers would kill 'emselves larfin'."

"You can look on, then, Uncle Dick."

"Yes, sar, massa; ole ooman an' myself tought how, if it wa'n't damp to-night, we would jist go out and take a look at 'em."

"I expect they will have a jolly time, Uncle Dick."

"When I was young, massa, I used to dance, and I tell yer what, no one couldn't beat dis nigger, but now I'se old, and don't care 'bout sich tings now. You ought jist to hab seen ole ooman and I; didn't we keep time wid de banjo doe?"

"It has been very long since that time, Uncle Dick. I judge so from the white hairs upon your head."

"O yes, massa; you see I'se been in de world a long time, and when de good Massa please to call me, den I will go to my home in heaben."

"I hope you will live a long time yet, Uncle Dick; but you know you are very old, and we cannot stay on earth always."

"Dat's true 'nough, massa; I stay as long as de good Massa please to lets me, and den when he calls, I go wid a chefful heart. Dar comes Rufus; I wonder what he wants wid me now. I 'spects he is comin' to talk 'bout de dance dey is gwine to hab to-night."

"Massa Charles, good mornin', sar. I hopes I sees yer well, dis mornin'."

"Very well, I thank you, Rufus. I was awakened

last night with some very pretty music; I think I heard your voice, Rufus."

Rufus hung down his head, and laughed. It always delighted him very much to have any one praise his singing.

"Massa, I come to tell yer dat we is gwine to hab a real plantation dance to-night."

"So I learned from Ben, this morning. I suppose you are one of the head ones there."

"Well, I is dat; I always takes de lead when dey gits up anyting ob de sort."

That day the slaves scarcely thought of anything else saving the dance, and each one determined in his own mind to acquit himself as well as possible. Never did the day pass more slowly away with them; they thought that night would never come.

But when they saw the sun setting, they all appeared very glad, and stopped their work, and were busy in making preparations.

"I tinks dis banjo is gwine to charm all de niggers to-night on dis plantation; it is dat. I bet it will make 'em all dance."

At the appointed time all took their places near the back porch. Charles and his parents took their seats, for the purpose of looking on. Charles was very much amused to see them all trying to do their best.

After a while the banjo struck. Now all were on tiptoe, dancing as if their life depended upon it. Ben screams out, "Ladies and gemmen, 'leomade all." From that they all went around at a great rate.

Charles was nearly convulsed with laughter, it really looked so new to him, for he had not seen anything of the kind for a long time; he of course enjoyed it exceedingly.

Rufus was grinning, and his heels were up as high as he could get them. Ben, too, was rolling up his eyes, and a broad grin would spread his mouth from ear to ear. Lizzie and Laura had danced until their tucking combs had fallen out of their hair. Uncle Dick and Aunt Phebe sat looking on, and were almost tempted to go on their heels.

"I tell yer what, ole ooman, dey is doin' dat dance bang up. Only jist look at dat foolish Rufus, wid his collar high 'nuff and stiff 'nuff to cut his throat, and it would sarve him right if it would jist sorter scratch him, for he is de most foolishest nigger I eber seed in all my life."

Charles heard the conversation between Aunt Phebe and Uncle Dick, and could scarcely suppress his laughter.

"Well, Charles," said Mr. M——, "what do you think of the dancing?"

"Oh! I am very much pleased with it indeed, and I really think all this merriment proceeds from the heart."

"I know it does; they talk about our slaves at the South, but I know, after all, that they are far better off, and more happy than the servants North."

"They are, certainly," said Charles; "for I was there for five years, but I never saw them so happy as our slaves are. I do wish a Northerner could get a glimpse of them; I know they would feel fully satisfied in their minds then, that our slaves are happy. It really does me good to see them all dancing at this rate. Are they in the habit of dancing often?"

"Yes; but they have not had a dance for two or three Saturday nights. I believe they have been in anticipation of this one; so they thought they would wait until you arrived home. They are all very glad indeed to see you."

"So it seems; I have been congratulated many times to-day by different ones. I am really glad to get home again, for I do think it is the happiest place in the world. It is true that I enjoyed myself very much at college, among the students, and liked the professors very much; but then that is not like being home. I shall be delighted when Dora comes; I do wonder what Aunt Phebe will say when she sees her; I know she will be perfectly delighted."

The slaves had been dancing for some time, and were now getting a little tired of it. So they all repaired to Aunt Phebe's cabin, for the purpose of taking refreshments. Charles received a very pressing invitation to the supper, but very respectfully declined, by saying that it had been but a little while since he had been to tea.

After they were all seated at the table, Charles went to take a peep at them. They all insisted upon his coming to the table; but he replied by saying that he only came to see how everything was coming on.

"We tanks yer berry much, massa, for yer being so good as to come and see us. We is gwine to dance one more jig before we all gibs up. We don't break down so fast."

Charles and his father sat in the porch, talking; they were waiting for the dancers to come out again.

" Here they come again," said Mr. M——; " I suppose they are about winding up now."

" Yes, I believe they intend to dance but one more reel !"

" Thump, thump, went the banjo ; now, all were on the go again, they get higher and higher. Ben calls out still louder, and they all go around without any ceremony whatever.

They kept it up about a half an hour, then slacked off; they all wished Charles good night, and then went to their cabins.

" I wonder what massa tinks ob de dance we had to night ! I seed him larfin', an' I 'specks he mighty glad. Didn't de ole banjo ring doe ?"

Each one, of course, thought he had acquitted himself the best, and wished they knew the opinion of their master.

" I 'specks he tinks he neber did see de like afore in his life. I likes to show 'em what dese darkies can do. He don't see none dis at de Norf, I knows berry well."

" No, dat he don't," said Rufus ; " dey all has to work too hard for any ting else."

" It's getting late, darkies, and I tell yer I tinks dat to-morrow we will all be right tired. I'se pretty nigh danced all dese feet off. One good ting, it's Sunday."

Aunt Phebe showed them that she did not feel disposed to have company in her cabin any longer, so they all took the hint and parted for the night.

CHAPTER XXI.

MR. M——'S ILLNESS—HIS RECOVERY—THE LETTER.

Two weeks after Charles' arrival at home, Mr. M——
went to visit his plantations on the other side of the
river for the purpose of giving directions in regard to
some cotton which was to be sent away. He returned
in about a week, and seemed in very good health and
spirits. About two days after he arrived home he was
taken suddenly very ill at twelve o'clock in the night.
What to do they could not divine, for Dr. L——, who
was their family physician, had been sent for that night
by one of his patients, and would not return till morning. The nearest physician was ten miles off. So
Charles went to the cabin of Rufus, and commenced
rapping at the door.

"Rufus, Rufus, hurry and dress yourself immediately.
Father is very ill, and you must go for Dr. N——; he
lives at least ten miles from here, and you must make
all possible haste; tell him not to delay a moment, for
I fear father is seriously ill."

"What seems to be de matter wid him, massa?"

"I don't know, Rufus, I think he has had a spasm."

"De Lor' bless me, yer don't say so. Jist wait till
I gits my shoes on, an' den I be off."

Rufus made all possible haste, and, in quite a little
while after he started, he was at Dr. N——'s.

While he was gone they were all waiting with much anxiety for the arrival of Dr. N——. Mr. M—— had had another spasm; and Mrs. M——, being naturally very timid, became nervous.

Old Aunt Phebe was making herself as useful as possible; she applied everything that would restore him. She insisted that her mistress should endeavor to compose herself, for she was really afraid it would cause her to be sick.

Charles was watching with much anxiety to see when Rufus and the doctor should arrive. Much to his gratification, he was there in less time than he expected. It happened the roads were good, and they could ride very fast. The physician entered the room where Mr. M—— was.

When he first looked at him, he appeared to be very doubtful, and shook his head.

No one saw this but Aunt Phebe, who told him to make everything appear as well as possible, for the sake of her mistress, who was very much distressed.

"What do you think is the matter, doctor?"

"I think his illness was caused by his being overheated; has he not been much in the sun lately?"

"Yes, sar, I b'lieve he has; he went to de tother plantation, an' I 'specks he rid too much in de sun."

"Well, you know the sun at this season of the year is very dangerous, it is so apt to give one the brain fever. I dare say, Mr. M—— has it, and great caution must be taken. All noise and excitement must be kept from him, and he must be as composed as possible."

"I will tend to all dat, doctor, an' I will tell missus. She has gone in de next room to get something. Dar she comes now!"

" Well, doctor, what do you think of Mr. M—— ?"

" Oh ! he is not seriously ill, and I think, with proper caution and attendance, he will escape a very severe attack of the brain or bilious fever."

" Dar, now, missus, jist keep yourself easy, 'caze I know dat de doctor does know."

" Yes, madam, I think you had better keep yourself composed, for your nerves are not very strong, and it is very apt to make you sick ; indeed, it might cause you to have a severe attack of the nervous fever."

" Do, missus, try and be composed ; mind what de doctor say, cause he knowed best."

" Doctor N—— remained there the rest of the night, seeing that Mr. M—— appeared to be so very ill, and he feared to leave him. Mrs. M—— was delighted to know that he would remain all night. Aunt Phebe sat up, notwithstanding the request of Mrs. M—— for her to retire.

" Yer doesn't tink, missus, dat I is gwine to go to bed, and leab yer here. No, dat I ain't; I'se gwine to sit jist whar I is."

" But I am a great deal younger than you are, Aunt Phebe."

" I knows dat, missus, but kin stand sottin' up better dan you."

Oh ! how long and tedious seemed the night to Mrs. M——, how gladly did she hail the first blush of morning, when she saw it coming smilingly forth from the East. It is only they who have watched by the couch of the sick who know what a gloom there is within that chamber at midnight. When morning came, Mr. M—— was much worse. The doctor forbid any one, saving his attendants, to enter the room; he feared that he might not again recover, but hoped that, with proper attention, he might.

When the slaves heard of the illness of their master, they were much alarmed, and feared lest he might never recover. Every little while some of them would go and inquire how he was. They were very anxious to go in his room; but, when they were told that it was the positive orders of the physician for all to be kept out of the room, they were still more frightened, and were even moved to tears.

Mrs. M—— scarcely knew what to do. She wanted to advise Dora of his illness, lest he might die, and then she would think it was very unkind in her mother not to tell her of his illness. Charles advised her to wait awhile, and see if he did not get better; and, if he did not, he would go to the city and have a telegraphic dispatch sent to her immediately. "It may," said he, "interfere with her studies; for I know so well what is her disposition." Upon the whole, they concluded not to tell her as yet. For some days, Mr. M—— was extremely ill; so much so, that they scarcely had any hopes of him at all. Happily, however, he began to mend a little, and they thought he would recover. He had less fever, and was not delirious, as he had been the preceding week.

One can well imagine the delight of Mrs. M——, when she saw her husband getting so much better, and when the physician told her that danger was past, and in a little while, if proper care was taken, he would be himself again.

One morning, after the change for the better had

taken place, Aunt Phebe went to her cabin for a few minutes, to prepare something for Mr. M——. Uncle Dick seeing her, asked how his master was.

"He is better, ole man; an' de doctor say he will git well 'gin."

"Tank de Lord for dat. I tell yer what, ole ooman, I'se been mighty 'feared all dis time dat massa would die; an' den what would we all do? You know dat woman can't do like man, nohow. Missus mought get some one to 'tend to tings for her, an' den dey would cheat her. I hopes to see massa up 'gin, dat I does."

"Where is old Uncle Dick?" inquired Mr. M—— one morning, after he got much better.

"He is in the cabin, I think, father. Do you wish to see him?"

"Yes, Charles; tell him to come in."

"Massa, how glad I is to see yer lookin' so smart; I does hope dat yer will git up 'gin. I was moughty 'feared dat yer was gwine ter die."

"I am thankful to the Good Being, Dick, that I am spared to my family. I want to see my daughter again, and I am anxious to see how Charles turns out."

"I does hope, massa, dat he will do well; an' I 'spects he will; for he is so good dat eberybody likes him, an' I does tink he will do well. Massa, you has been mighty sick."

"Yes, very sick, Dick; but I am a great deal better. You see I overheated myself; the sun was very warm, indeed, and I rode about a great deal, attending to my business."

"I tought dat yer would make yerself sick; I tol' ole ooman so de tother day, when I heerd you say dat you was gwine away. You has been sick 'some time, nearly four weeks."

"I have suffered a good deal, indeed; the doctor thinks I was threatened with the brain fever."

"I hopes, massa, dat yer will take better care ob yourself next time. I must go now, 'caze I feel sorter tired; an' I tinks if yer will take a good nap, yer will feel better. I will come agin."

"You must, Dick; I shall be glad to see you."

"De Lord be praised," said Uncle Dick, after he went into his cabin; "massa is gettin' well, ole ooman. I'se mighty glad, I tells yer."

"Yer ain t no gladder dan I is."

"I don't 'specks I is."

"I must run in de house now, wid de plaster; dey is waitin' for me."

Dora had been wondering at the long silence of her father for some time; she attributed it, though, to his being very busy; but when he delayed writing so long, she became very uneasy. "I wonder mother does not write," said she; "I fear something is the matter at home."

It had been more than a month since Mr. M—— was taken ill. He was now getting entirely well; so the first time he felt able, he wrote to Dora. He knew it had been a long time since she had heard from him, so he determined to write. One day, feeling unusually better, he wrote:—

"MY DEAR DAUGHTER:—

"You wonder, no doubt, at my long silence; and when I tell you the cause of it, you will see that it was not without a good cause. I have been extremely ill, but Providence has kindly spared me. I am quite feeble, as yet, but I am very much better, and can now leave my room. The doctor said I was threatened with the brain fever, but happily I escaped it. I feel very grateful, my dear daughter, when I reflect that I am still spared, and hope that I may see you once more. I thought of you much during my illness, and wished that you could have been with me. Aunt Phebe was very attentive during my illness; she is a fond, faithful servant, and I intend to set her and Uncle Dick free at some future time. I mentioned to them once that I intended setting them free, and they said they did not desire it; but I still intend giving them their freedom. I hope you will acquit yourself admirably at the coming examination, and that I shall have as much cause to feel proud as I did when your brother graduated. Study hard and faithfully, my dear daughter, and I am confident that you will succeed. Do not be uneasy about me in the least, for I am almost entirely well. Your mother and brother are both well, and so are all the slaves. Write to me soon, for I am anxious to hear from you.

"Adieu, my dear daughter.

"Your devoted father,

"T. A. M."

Mr. M—— sealed the letter, and sent it immediately, for he was anxious that she should get it as soon as possible. He continued to get much better, and in a little while was out again. Aunt Phebe and Uncle Dick begged him not to go in the sun, and to take good care of himself. The physician had said there was danger of a relapse if caution was not taken. So Mr. M—— was very prudent, and his health became as good as usual in a little while.

To those who have been confined to the couch of sickness, how delightful it is to be up again; how lovely everything in nature appears, particularly in the autumn. There is something so extremely sad in that season; the falling of the leaves seem to whisper that everything in nature is passing away. It had been two months since Mr. M—— left his room ; never did the air feel more balmy, or nature's garb look more lovely. He gazed upon all these beauties, and felt grateful that he was spared upon earth a longer time ; he thought it was for some wise purpose. Mr. M—— was a man of piety, and saw Providence in everything.

When Madora received her father's letter it made her feel very sad; he feared that he might take a relapse, yet hoped he would not. For his sake she studied and determined to acquit herself well at the coming examination. She thought of her brother, and hoped that she also might meet with the same success ; and if studying would do it, she intended to make every effort possible. She had become more and more a favorite of the teachers in consequence of her deportment and diligence. Time passed on with her less heavily than she anticipated ; it was just as Lydia had told her, for her studies had so engrossed her attention that she had not time to think of much else but them. Day after day she applied herself with zeal, and won the esteem and love of all around her.

CHAPTER XXII.

DORA AGAIN—THE EXAMINATION—PLEASANT TOUR.

Dora had applied herself according to the injunction laid upon her by her brother when they parted. Now the time appointed for the final examination was at hand. She had prepared her lessons, yet with all this a fear would come over her at times when she reflected upon the examination. She had received many encouraging letters from her parents, who urged her to press on, and lay aside all fear.

"In a few days," thought she, "I shall see them again. Oh! how happy I shall be, too; for they have promised me a nice pleasure trip, and I shall really feel like a bird out of a cage. To think that six long years have passed since I was home. Oh! how my heart yearns to be there again; there is no spot half so dear to me. Oh, no! I would not leave that genial clime to dwell in any of the far-famed isles, but give me my sunny home and I am content. How things have changed, and how I have changed, too, with them; from a little child, I have grown into womanhood. Yet, amid all this, I forget not the home of my childhood; each tree, each flower is dear to me; and how my heart throbs with the same joy to see that loved spot as when first I left it. Many are the warm hearts which throb for me, and I return all the affection which emanates from so pure a source."

Dora had taken her seat at the foot of a favorite tree, for the purpose of studying her lessons for the great day which was to decide for her whether she would or would not acquit herself honorably. She studied until the sun had set; and now she laid her book aside to indulge in her own reflections. Near the tree was a stream all sparkling and beautiful, tall grass fringed its borders, and at early morn a diamond would rest upon each blade. Dora loved that spot because it was so romantic and beautiful; when she wished to write her essays she would go there, for she thought that the most meet place; there she saw nature in her most lovely form. Dora felt a little sad when she reflected that she should so soon leave school. She loved the teachers and pupils, but yet she loved her home more than all; she felt that none were so kind to her, and no smile was like that of a mother's.

The day of the final examination came. Dora had the highest honors conferred upon her. Her parents and brother were there, together with a great number of spectators.

When she turned to address her classmates, tears started down her cheeks as the words—" and to you, my classmates, I must say 'adieu;' long have we studied together and drank of the fountains of knowledge. We part, and time alone will decide whether or not we meet again; but, in yon bright heaven there is one who knoweth all things, and even now looks down upon us. Angels, too, watch over and guide our footsteps; may they ever keep us in the path of rectitude, and whisper to us our duty. Many links in the chain of affection may be severed, but let us hope to have them again united in heaven. We go to our own homes; some to the 'sunny South,' where softest breezes waft their sweet perfume from magnolia vales, and where flowers shed their softest fragrance; others to a less genial clime to cheer the fireside of aged parents. I would not say 'adieu,' but time speeds on and on, every moment brings the parting hour nearer. But we will not forget these classic halls; no, no, too dear are they held in memory! We shall ever think of our kind instructors, who have toiled with us during our ascent up the steep hill of science. Classmates, once more, farewell; may Heaven ever smile graciously upon you all, and may your pathway in life be ever strewn with flowers. The time has come for us to part, and we now must say 'adieu.'"

Charles had been listening with fixed attention to his sister's essay, and tears fell from his eyes.

The whole assemblage was struck with the pathos in which she uttered every word, music seemed to breathe in every line; it was, indeed, read with much feeling and expression. The whole room rang with applauses; and when she finished reading her essay a thousand congratulations were showered upon her. Every one was asking, who is that young lady that read the valedictory; was it not eloquent, was it not touching?

Charles heard the various compliments which were passed upon his sister, and was very much pleased, as it was very natural he should be. He thought she never looked more beautiful or innocent.

There was a childlike simplicity about Dora which was very pleasing. She had not those airs which many boarding-school girls possess, particularly after leaving school, nor was there any of that self-importance and desire to show off to the greatest extent imaginable. She was the admiration of those who saw her, and her society was courted by all.

Dora, the childlike being whom we introduced to our readers at the beginning of the book, had now as it were undergone a complete change. Now, she was a woman in every sense of the word, invested with that high dignity of character which made her appear so lovely.

Mr. M—— almost idolized his daughter, and feared lest he should love her too much.

"I do wonder what Aunt Phebe will say when she sees you, Dora? You are my sister, and I know I ought not to tell you, but, I declare, you are a perfect Juno. I never saw any one improve so much as you have in my life; but you bid fair from a child to be a pretty woman?"

"Now, Charles, for mercy's sake, do not commence flattering me, I am not susceptible of it. I know very well that I have many weak points, but that does not happen to be one of them. I know young gentlemen think that nothing is more pleasant to the ladies than to flatter them; but, I do assure you, I am not fond of it at all; it is no music in my ear."

"Now, sister, that is just like you; if we happen to pay a compliment, when it is deserved, to the ladies, they say directly that we are flattering them. You just wait until Aunt Phebe sees you."

"Dear old soul! I do wonder what she will say? I expect she will be overjoyed; she will scarcely know how to contain herself. I shall see her, I hope, in a little while. How long shall we be gone to the Springs, Charles?"

"I do not know exactly, but I suppose about three months. I do not think it will be prudent for you to go South so soon; it is August now, and you will be travelling until October."

"No, I should not think so. Has it been healthy there this season?"

"Yes, quite so; but then I would not like to have you risk going there so soon."

"But I should not think it would be pleasant at the springs so late."

"We will not stay there too late; we will go to some of the Northern cities, and stay there until it is time for us to go home."

"Madora, have you everything in readiness?" asked Mr. M——.

"Not quite, papa."

"Well, make haste, my dear; for we must leave in about an hour from now."

Off Dora went, to get everything in readiness, and in a little while she was prepared to start.

Oh! how happy does the scholar feel when she knows that she has done herself and her instructors honor; when she has pleased her anxious parents. Oh! how delightful the thought that she is released from school, and can now be free from study.

Dora was charmed, indeed. Never did the scenes around her look more beautiful, although she had travelled that way every summer since she left her home. It was the thought of being free from school, and of returning home. Oh! beautiful and bright were her anticipations for the future.

They soon arrived at F——. Here was a scene so different from what Dora had been participating in; nothing but gayety, gayety, gayety. She met with some friends there, and it made time pass off more pleasantly. She compared her feelings to a bird which had passed through the cold storms of winter, and warbles forth a song because spring has returned. Dora had no longer any pallor, but two bright roses blushed upon her cheek, and she was in the full vigor of health and beauty. Her conversation delighted all with whom she met, and her amiability and meekness won their admiration. Dora felt that she had been amply repaid for all the sad feelings which she experienced at boarding-school; and, if she had given up to them, and gone home, she would have regretted it all her life.

At all the most fashionable watering-places she was proclaimed the belle, and a countless number of admirers were around her; but she had given her heart to another, and determined to prove constant to her first love. Although she created so much sensation, yet she was devoid of that vanity which sometimes shows itself so plainly in some of the reigning belles of the day; every one who saw her made that observation. Her dress was always simple and becoming, her manners retiring, her conversation well chosen. It was not her ambition to eclipse others, yet she did so. She was, indeed, a bright planet, surrounded by many satellites.

Dora felt that Heaven had indeed smiled upon and blessed her; and she was grateful to the Good Being for thus permitting her to enjoy the luxuries of life. She fully intended to put her wealth to the best possible use, for she knew that the day would come when she should have to give an account of it. From her earliest years she envied a benevolent spirit, and, as she grew up, it continued. Nothing could afford her more pleasure than to administer to the wants of the needy, and she made it a rule never to turn off a beggar. But we have been saying so much about her virtues, that we have almost forgotten her trip.

Dora remained at the springs about eight weeks; she then went to visit some of the Northern cities, and take a general view of the different places. She was quite anxious to get home, but would not say anything to her parents, lest it might interfere with their wishes; for she knew very well that they would do anything she desired.

"Well, Dora," said Mr. M—— one day, "how were you pleased with your trip?"

"Very much delighted, papa. Really, I have had a charming time of it. I have been very happy this summer, and I never felt better in my life."

"I never saw you look better. I was just thinking what Aunt Phebe would say to those roses on your cheeks. I remember I wrote you word that she said she would never believe they were there until she saw them."

"It will be quite an agreeable disappointment to her. I scarcely know how she will contain herself."

"I really do not think she will know you."

"No, indeed, she will not," said Charles; "for—"

"Now, just hush, brother; for I do not wish you to commence flattering me."

"So you have been flattering your sister, have you, Charlie?"

"No, father; I was only telling her the truth, and she will not believe me."

"I'll wager that Dora is pretty well versed in the ways of young gentlemen, if she has been at boarding-school, where they are not allowed even to see one. I imagine she has some little bird who whispers all these things to her."

"But she must not judge all the world alike."

"No, I don't, Charlie; but I know you so well."

"I think you will find me out better after you have been with me a little while."

"I think," said Mr. M——, "that it is time we were thinking about getting home; what say the rest of the party? Majority rules, you know."

"I second the motion," said Dora; "I have been quite anxious to go for several weeks, but I did not say anything about it, lest it might interfere with your plans; and then my wishes might have interrupted them."

"We will, then, agree upon starting to-morrow. I am heartily anxious to get home."

"I want to see the meeting between Aunt Phebe and sister."

"I imagine it will exceed that of yours with Uncle Dick."

"I know it will; I dare say Aunt Phebe has looked for us until she is tired."

"We will determine on starting to-morrow, if it is the wish of all the company," replied Mr. M——.

Early the next morning, agreeably to the wishes of Dora, they all left for the "sunny South."

CHAPTER XXIII.

DORA'S RETURN HOME—MEETS AUNT NELLY'S GRAVE—
HER FEELINGS.

THE journey really seemed very long to Dora, for she was anxious to get home. She insisted that her father should not stop any more on the way than he could possibly help. At the expiration of two weeks, she beheld her own home.

"Oh! how natural," exclaimed she, "do all the little cabins look. There is Aunt Phebe's; I do wonder what she will say when she sees me?"

Aunt Phebe had been ironing; she expected they would be home that day, so she hurried with her work. Hearing a carriage coming, she went to the door.

"Dar dey come; I tole yer so, ole man."

In a moment, Aunt Phebe had Dora in her arms.

"De Lors bless me, if yer ain't growed the purtiest ting dat yer eber seed in my life. Oh! bless dis chil', bless dis chil'! Aunt Phebe neber 'spected to see yer 'gin, and now yer stand afore her; tank de Lord for dis."

Aunt Phebe wept freely; she was so overjoyed that she could not refrain from giving vent to her feelings. Dora had not been so much caressed for a long time. She highly appreciated it all, and felt that Aunt Phebe was a true and faithful friend.

21

In a minute, almost, every slave on the plantation knew she had come. Uncle Dick went hobbling along as well as he could.

"Jist look, ole ooman, at dat ar' face; jist see dem red cheeks; didn't dey tell yer so? yer b'lieves, now, don't yer?"

"Dat I does; I hope dey will stay dat way all de time. Dat don't look like Miss Dora, nohow."

"Well, ole ooman, don't yer know dat she habs grown? When she fust went from us, she wa'n't no bigger dan a grasshopper."

"I knowed dat; but somehow I tinks she looks purtier dan she did den."

"Sure she do. Look at dem dar cheeks, will yer."

"Who is this?" said Dora, pointing to Lizzie; I never saw her before."

"It is Benjamin's wife, my dear; she formerly belonged to Mr. B——. You have forgotten her; she came to assist about your clothes, when you were getting ready to go away to school."

"O yes! I recollect that you had some one to help you sew them, mamma. So, this is Lizzie."

"Yes, marm, missus. I'se mighty glad to see yer; when I made yer dresses, yer wa'n't no bigger dan nothin'."

"Where is Ben, the one who used to play on the banjo?"

"Here's me, missus. I kin play to eberyting you eber heered in your life. I makes dese niggers tink dat de debble is tickling on dere heels sometimes."

"So, you have improved very much in playing, then."

"O yes, missus, berry much; I kin do de ting bang up, I tell yer, since massa fotched me dat new banjo."

"This is your wife, Ben. I declare, you have made a nice bargain."

From this Lizzie commenced to titter, and seemed to think she was the prettiest person in the world.

"Here is my wife," said Rufus, bringing Laura forward.

"So, this is Laura. Well, I declare, you have all had a great number of weddings since I left. Where are John, Thomas, Moses, Carey, and the other slaves? I want to see them all."

"I s'pects dey is in de cabin, fixin' up."

"Well, I will take a look at the cabins as soon as I get rested."

"You must come to mine, missus," said Ben. "I'se got a splendid one, an' de purtiest little chil' you eber did see."

"Very well; I will come."

Those who have been absent a long time from home, and see many changes when they return, can judge of the feelings of Dora. Aunt Nelly was gone; and she sighed when she thought of her.

"My home, my home, my happy home!" said Dora. "Oh! how I love it. Blest scenes of my childhood, fain would I wander amid them again. But, ah! it has all passed away. The tall grass has grown upon the grave of Aunt Nelly, just as she told me. I will visit her grave; she lies by the side of little Hannah now, but her spirit is in heaven. She was a good old Christian, and I sigh when I think that I shall see her no more on earth; but I hope to meet her in heaven. Everything around looks familiar to me; those tall oaks flourish still, and look as green as ever. With the exception of marriage and death, very little change has taken place."

One morning, Dora went to the cabin of Aunt Phebe, and asked her to go with her that afternoon to visit the grave of Aunt Nelly.

"Dat I will, honey. I will finish my work, an' go wid you."

Afternoon came, and Aunt Phebe and Dora went to visit the grave. How Dora wept; there was such a silence around. The weeping-willow was waving its branches; the jasmine, which Uncle Dick had planted, still bloomed as beautifully as ever; the grass had grown tall, and a few blue violets might be seen smiling, and wafting their fragrance around.

"Poor old Aunt Nelly lies here now; she told me she should, when I left. She said I must come to her grave, for she should be lying by the side of little Hannah. I should have liked to see her again, but I never shall on earth. I trust that I shall meet her in heaven, for I know she has gone there."

"Dat she has, honey; for if dar eber was a Christian gone home to glory, she has gone. I seed 'nuff ob her to know."

"She died very happy, I believe, Aunt Phebe?"

"Yes, missus, dat she did; and she spoke of you. Oh! I felt when I seed her gwine, an' tought dat if I was only gwine, too; but den I knowed dat de good Massa will call me when he pleases."

"I feel sorry when I think that poor old Aunt Nelly is dead; but then I know she is much better off."

"Dat she is, for she was wellnigh worn out when she lef' us; an' I tought den dat she was gwine home to heaben."

Dora stood there thoughtfully, and wept; although Aunt Nelly was a slave, yet she felt as much affection for her as if she had been white.

"Missus, why does yer grieve? Yer was a mighty good chil' to her, an' she loved yer so good. She always told me yer was good to her, an' dat I must tell you to meet her in de land ob promise."

It was now twilight. Never in her life did Dora feel more sad. She was standing by the grave of two departed beings, on the very spot where she stood just six years ago. Oh! what a host of recollections crowded upon her mind. She heard the notes of a little bird while she stood there, and she said, "Aunt Phebe, perhaps that is the spirit of Aunt Nelly, whispering to me now."

"Yes, missus, I tinks so, too; 'caze I does b'lieve dat Nelly is in heaben dis bery ebening."

"My childhood's home!" mused Dora. "Oh! how dear it is to me. How beautiful and how natural does every object appear. Gladly do I welcome it; and I feel that I love no place so well. A few months since, I was among many who were my friends in name, but I fear there were but few in heart; now I am in the midst of those who, I know, love me. I should be happy; yes, I am happy, and feel grateful to Heaven for having thus blessed me."

Aunt Phebe, seeing Dora standing so silently, and looking so sad, said, " Missus, I tinks yer had better go now, for it's gittin' late, an' yer feel so bad. I don't like to see yer lookin' dat way. Please, marm, look more chee'ful afore you go whar missus is, 'caze yer will make her feel mighty bad if yer looks dat way."

They now started, and in a little while were at home.

" Where have you been, my dear?" asked her mother.

" To Aunt Nelly's grave."

" That is why you look so sad."

" I feel sad, mamma; I cannot refrain from it; for it brought to memory scenes of the past, when I was but a child."

" Reflections are very apt to make us feel sad sometimes, but you must overcome all this. I have often noticed that you are in the habit of thinking too much. You must endeavor to avoid it, or it will make you feel very unhappy."

" No, dear mamma, you need not fear that; I shall be quite gay again after a little while. You know that I have got home, and the recollection of having parted with my teachers and classmates, besides having just been to Aunt Nelly's grave, is calculated to make me feel sad. It is only momentary, and I do not intend to get in any such moods again; I am going to banish it altogether."

" That is a good resolution, my dear; and I hope you will follow it all through life. Determine to be happy in whatever situation you may be placed, and I am sure that life will glide on more smoothly with you."

After Aunt Phebe had left Dora, she went about supper; Uncle Dick was sitting in the cabin when she came in.

"Whar has yer been, ole ooman, I ain't seed yer sence dinner?"

"I'se been to de grave of Nelly. Yer know dat Miss Dora wanted ter go, and she axed me to go wid her. Ole man, I do wish yer could hab seed her, it would hab done yer heart good, I tell yer; she cried jist like a baby. I always tole yer dat ebery body lubed her; I knowed it."

"I knowed dat she lubed ole ooman, Nelly."

"Yes, dat she does; an' if yer had jist seed her cryin' at de grave, yer would tought so. I'se gwine to hurry wid supper, 'caze I wants ter talk to her a little bit."

Aunt Phebe bustled around, and soon got tea ready.

After tea, agreeably to her wishes, she had an opportunity of having a talk with Dora, who kindly accepted the invitation of Aunt Phebe to visit her cabin to see how she was getting on, and to give her a word of praise about her cake and family rolls. It had been a long time since she had sat there with Aunt Phebe; but everything looked familiar to her, although it was six years since she had been home.

CHAPTER XXIV.

THE SURPRISE—THE VISIT—DORA—MORE ABOUT AUNT
PHEBE AND UNCLE DICK.

THE reader will probably remember that the day on which Lydia bade adieu to R——, she left Dora with her brother in the arbor, while she was getting in readiness. Much passed between them, for Harry had fallen deeply in love with Dora since he first met her at Niagara. He thought no being so lovely as herself; he admired her childlike simplicity and innocency. Dora felt an attachment for him; and they would have corresponded, had it not been against the rules of school for any young man to hold any communication whatever with a young lady by letter. It was a very wise rule, too, for it might else have served to divert the mind of the student from her studies; and, besides, prove of no advantage in the end.

Harry had determined that, so soon as she should have completed her studies, he would make his proposals to her; yet he had many delicate feelings upon the subject. He knew that she was wealthy, and feared lest her parents might think this his aim. But that was the farthest thought from his mind; for when he first saw Dora, he fell in love with her, and he knew nothing of her wealth then.

Dora often thought of him while at school, and looked

forward to the time that she should meet him, with great pleasure.

Before he left R—— (on the morning of which we introduced him to our reader as sitting in the arbor), he expressed his sentiments freely and fully to Dora; and at the same time intimated the pleasure which it would afford him to write to her, but he knew that the rules of the school would not permit. He desired her to think of him kindly, and assured her that his attachment for her was very great, and that he regarded the circumstances which led them to meet with delight, and thought it had paved the way for his future happiness. She was the angel of his daydreams, and the vision of beauty which haunted his sleeping hours. Dora was all on earth to him; and to see her, be with her, was all he desired; the greatest bliss he would ask for.

Long indeed did the months seem to her; while Dora was at school; and, could she have had her wish, she would have hastened time onward.

When he heard of the success with which she met at the examination, and the beauty of the address she delivered, he felt as though she were almost a supernatural being. Circumstances were such that he could not attend the examination; he was compelled to go to some place to transact business for his father, which could not be delayed by any means whatever. He had anticipated going, but was disappointed, sadly, when he found it impossible for him to attend. He desired to see Dora on that memorable day, for he felt confident that success would be hers. Her fame was spread abroad, and Harry was the first one who heard how she acquitted herself. Oh, what feelings of pride and pleasure sprang up in his bosom when he heard it! He would rather that she would have been in possession of a laurelled name than to have won it himself; and in her was concentrated all his hopes, all his affections.

Dora returned all his devotion really and truly, she saw something so noble and elevated about him; his very countenance was intellect itself. There was that frank and open expression about him which would almost enable one to read his character directly. His taste was fine, and of the first order; he was a devoted lover of music, and admired it from the most simple notes of the waterfall to the lofty organ peals. There was such a congeniality existing between the two that it is not wonderful that love should have sprung up between them.

Since Dora's arrival home, she had thought of him very often, and was never happier than when she received his letters.

Harry anticipated visiting her, but he did not advise her of it, because he wished to take her by surprise. Dora wondered that he did not pay her a visit, but did not expect it, by any means; for she thought that, if he had any intention of coming, he would have mentioned it in his letters to her. At times she would get distrustful, and think he did not care for her; but often she would console herself with the idea that business prevented him from paying her a visit. She looked sad; but always, in the presence of her mother, she would have a smile, in order to disguise her real feelings, for fear of rendering her mother unhappy. She felt it her duty to contribute as much to the welfare of her mother as possible, and determined that she would do it at the risk of everything.

Her brother was in the habit of taking her riding every morning, on horseback, for he thought it would be beneficial to her. The air at the South, in autumn, is very delightful; it is neither warm nor cold; it resembles an Indian-summer. One morning they rode a good distance, much farther than they were aware of. They happened to look a little to the right of the road, and saw some one on horseback.

"Look, brother, there is some one else riding. I do wonder who it is? I cannot distinguish whether there is a lady in company, or not; but we shall see directly."

The person approached nearer and nearer, until at last he could be seen distinctly.

"Oh! it is Lydia's brother, Charlie, I do believe."

"No, you must be mistaken, I think."

"I am certain it is he. Yes, yes, I am right—I know I am."

"We will stop a few minutes, until he gets nearer, and we can tell then."

The rider advanced, and, sure enough, it was Harry. What could exceed Dora's surprise? She could scarcely realize that she saw him; it was so unexpected.

"Good-morning to you both," said Harry. "I was just coming out to your house. Really, I am delighted that I have met you on the road."

"We were just on the eve of turning back for home. We have gone much farther than we expected."

"Then I will accompany you."

"We shall be delighted to have you do so. But stop, here is a spring, and we will have a little chat, and get a drink of this delightful water. Here are some large leaves."

"Really, Miss Dora, I never saw you looking better in my life; why your cheeks are as near like roses as they can be, and as smiling as a May morning."

The surprise and excitement of meeting Harry had caused a deeper blush to mantle her cheeks, and her eyes sparkled brighter, too. Her riding-habit was extremely becoming; it consisted of a clove-colored merino, which fitted her form exquisitely; a straw flat, around which was placed a simple band of ribbon, with a bow and ends, which fell gracefully upon her shoulders. Her whip consisted of whalebone, mounted with gold, and she flourished it with much grace, tapping the water in the spring, or rustling it amid the leaves of the trees around.

"Really, you remind me of Lady Gay Spanker. Come, give us a description of 'the chase,' and I shall really imagine it is her."

Dora, after being much persuaded, recited it for the gratification of Harry. Julia Dean or Mrs. Stuart could not have surpassed her. There was so much ease about her manner and gesture. Harry really looked upon her with admiration, for she exceeded his expectations.

"I think," said Charles, "that we had better make our way home again; for we have quite a distance to go yet, and I fear the sun will get too warm. You know, Dora, that you are not used to this climate yet, for you have been away so long. I would not have you run any risk until you are well acclimated. I notice very often that you seem debilitated."

"Oh! that is only in the heat of the day."

"Well, if you were accustomed to the climate you would not feel so, or if your constitution were strong."

"Allow me," said Harry, "to assist you, Miss Dora, in mounting your horse."

"With pleasure," replied Dora.

"Here are the reins. Wait a minute, and we will start; our horses have rested, and we shall go the swifter for it."

"How far have we to go?"

"About six miles."

"That is not quite so far as I thought we had to go."

"We shall soon get there; for the horses seem very spirited, and I think we shall go very swiftly."

"These are very fine specimens of Southern horses," observed Harry.

"Yes, very fine, indeed. We Southerners always did boast of our horses."

"By the by, Miss Dora, what do you call yours?"

"Marie Stuart."

"A pretty name, I declare. I admire your choice in the selection; and, were I at a loss for a name, I should certainly call upon you to choose for me."

"You are in a very complimentary mood this morning, Mr. B——."

"Oh! not more than usual; I never compliment only when I think it is deserved, and I am sure it is in your case."

"I was just thinking, Mr. B——, how you managed to find the way out here."

"I had an attendant; he happened to see Charles, and told me that was the person of whom I was in quest;

22

so I told him he need go no farther with me, then ; that I would keep on with you."

" A fortunate meeting it was."

"And a very pleasant one, too !"

" Here we are!" said Charles.

" Are we there, really ?   I had no idea that we were so near."

" No, I suppose not; you and sister have had a complete *tête-à-tête*, and I could only play the part of listener."

" What are all those little houses, and who are all those people around them ?   This part of the country is quite new to me, for I have never travelled this way before."

" That is the negro quarter, and those people you speak of are slaves."

"Slaves ?"

"Yes, slaves!"

" They seem to be having a merry time, indeed."

" They are a happy set I assure you ; and if you stay here long enough they will give you a fair demonstration of the fact.   They generally welcome all strangers by giving them a serenade.   It would really amuse you to see them."

" I wonder what keeps our equestrians so long this morning," observed Mrs. M——.   " It is past breakfast time, and they have not made their appearance yet. I suppose they have met with a very agreeable detention on the road, or they would have been here before this time ; but there is one advantage, they will have a better appetite when they come."

"Here they are now," said Mr. M——; "there are three; you see they have added one to their number since they left. I thought something more than usual had occurred; the air has, no doubt, done them much good. Just look at Dora's cheeks, they are as rosy as if they had been painted. I think the ride has done her good."

They all alighted from their horses, and went towards the house; Dora and Harry in front.

"Oh! I see now who it is they have met with; do you not remember the young gentleman whom she met at Niagara Falls? he is the brother to the young lady whom Dora was so intimate with at boarding-school. I do wonder where they happened to meet him?"

Charles, after renewing the introduction of Harry to his parents, left the room for a few minutes to attend to having the horses fed and put in the stable. Harry, Dora, and her father now formed the company, Mrs. M—— having gone to make some arrangements about breakfast.

"I had really forgotten your favor, Mr. B——," said Mr. M——; "I thought I had seen your face before, when I saw you coming, but I could not tell exactly where I had seen you. You know that I am getting advanced in life now, and my memory is not so good as when I was younger. Where did you all meet?"

"I was on my way here, and I happened to meet Miss Dora and her brother; so I dismissed my attendant, and told him that I would return with them."

"We are very happy to welcome you here, sir!"

"I suppose you all must have a good appetite after your morning's ride, for it is now quite late."

"I breakfasted before I started."

"You must have had a very early breakfast, then; it is, however, two hours after our usual time, but we thought we would wait until our equestrians arrived."

Rufus, now as polite as a dancing-master, came into the room and announced that breakfast was waiting.

Mr. M—— invited Harry; he declined at first, but they all insisted so much upon his going in, that he soon found there was no alternative but to accept the invitation.

"You all met with quite an adventure this morning. I suppose you have enjoyed yourselves very much indeed?"

"We did, and we had a drink of delightful spring water, it was so cool and clear; I do believe I have felt invigorated ever since I drank it."

"I am extremely happy to know that it has benefited you, Miss Dora, and feel honored that I filled the agreeable office of handing it to you."

"I noticed your cheeks looked very blooming when you came in, Dora, and thought that something more than usual must have pleased you. You had a delightful morning for the ride!"

"I think I never saw more charming weather for this season of the year," said Harry. "It is so unlike the cold freezing weather of my own home. Why, it is a perfect Indian-summer here; and, although it is quite late in autumn, not a leaf scarcely has fallen. Nature looks as beautiful almost as it did in early spring. When I left L——, it was cold enough for fires; in fact, we have had frost several times. I would give anything to live in such a climate as this. I am sure I should be perfectly happy. I have often read and heard of the beauty of the 'sunny South,' but this is the first time I have had an opportunity of testing it. Do you have such fine weather all winter?"

"We do not have it quite so warm as it is now, but it is very moderate."

"It is really a treat for me to enjoy such balmy air at this season."

There were a great many trees around the dwelling of Mr. M——, which shaded it beautifully. During the heat of the day it was even pleasant.

After they had breakfasted, Dora, with her brother, took Harry around to see the cabins and the different parts of the plantation. He was very much infatuated with the place, and felt as though he were in a perfect paradise. The conservatory was filled with the most choice flowers; the perfume was regaling to the senses as they entered; it was almost like going to an elysium.

· Charles left Dora and Harry in there to rest themselves, while he went to give some directions to the overseer of the plantation.

The absence of Charles was not lamented by the remaining party; it was quite the contrary.

Harry thought this a meet place to express his sentiments to Dora, surrounded by flowers from which was wafted the most regaling fragrance. The birds in the cages seemed to forget their captivity, and now poured forth their sweetest songs. A meet time, now at morning, when the sun shone brightly in heaven's blue arch; not one cloud marred the beauty; a balmy breeze, too, left its haunts to shed its genial influence upon the glad pair. The youthful happy creatures were seated side by side, and their hearts beat truly and warmly for each other.

Not long had they been alone ere Harry made known his intentions to Dora. He had come to express the wish of his heart, and to appoint the day when they should be married. Dora consented to his proposal, and Harry was intensely happy.

It was agreed that they should be united in the bands of wedlock in the spring; and as Harry looked forward to that time, he thought it a very long period to be separated from the object of his heart.

"I leave you," said Harry, "dear Dora, in a few days, but I will ever be with you in spirit, for I fondly love you. Would that I could remain till spring, but business demands that I should be at home at a certain time, else I would not leave you."

The time had passed so pleasantly that they had no idea it was so late. They heard a bell ringing.

"That cannot be the dinner-bell, surely," said Dora.

"I do not think it is late; but let me see what time it is?"

"Dear me! it is three o'clock."

"Ah! Dora, we have not been taking any heed of time; at least, I have not; for I was so agreeably entertained that I had forgotten all about it."

"So had I; but come, let us go; for there comes Charles, now."

"You must have had quite a *tête-à-tête*. I declare, you have been here since eleven o'clock this morning."

"Oh! well, we have not been at all at a loss how to amuse ourselves, or we should not have remained so long."

When they reached the house, they all had a hearty laugh at them for spending so long a time in the conservatory, and wondered what they had to talk about of so much importance.

The few days that Harry remained at Mr. M——'s, he thought certainly were the happiest of his life; and when the time came for him to take his departure, he felt a great reluctance in bidding adieu to Dora. It was perfectly natural that he should feel thus. Dora had shed many secret tears about his intended departure, and she wished that it were possible for him to remain longer.

Harry left in about three days after his arrival, and expressed the pleasure which his visit had afforded him.

Reader, have you ever seen the parting between two lovers? Could you not fancy you heard the throbbings of their hearts? Have you not watched their desponding looks? If so, you can judge what were the feelings of Dora and Harry. But they were cheered with a bright hope; for when spring came they would meet again, and a happy meeting it would be; for then they would not be separated again.

After the departure of Harry, Dora looked quite disconsolate; she would often go to the conservatory and sit for an hour or two, and reflect upon that eventful morning on which she had exchanged sentiments with Harry. As winter came, she felt still more lonely; and although she had any quantity of visitors, yet the right one was not there. But time, which must wear away all things, allayed, in a measure, her grief; and it was only when she reflected very deeply upon Harry, that she felt sad. But the continued entreaties of her mother, who urged her to wear a smiling face, and the hope of what spring would bring to her, served to make her quite happy again.

CHAPTER XXV.

VISIT FROM LYDIA—DORA'S MARRIAGE—AUNT PHEBE
AND UNCLE DICK—SUMMARY.

SPRING came—bright, joyous spring, when nature as
it were awakens from her dormant state, and rejoices;
the flowers bloom, and everything puts on its brightest
livery. Oh! how happy was Dora, for she was in anticipation of such an important event. Lydia, too, had
come to make her a visit, and now all was happiness
again for Dora. Lydia was to be her first bridesmaid,
and she was so delighted at the idea of calling Dora
" sister."

During the winter Dora had been quite gay; that is
to say, considering circumstances. There were a great
many persons around, and they all seemed to take quite
a fancy to Dora. She was the leading star wherever
she went.

It appeared that she had made an impression on more
hearts than one; but she could not give hers in exchange, for one already shared it.

The day appointed for the arrival of Harry came.
Dora and Lydia were looking out of the window, and
they happened to see him coming. What a sensation
it must have produced when Dora first beheld him! It
was only a week before her wedding, and she thought
of the responsible step which she was about to take.

We will not stop to note every little particular and event which transpired during that time, but will take our readers to the day on which Dora was to be married.

Everything was in elegance; the most sumptuous fare was provided, and it was more like the feast of a queen than anything else.

Aunt Phebe had been busy a month or two, preparing jellies, and other sweetmeats, and every indispensable. The most choice wines were purchased, and no pains or expense whatever was spared for the occasion.

The hour for Dora's marriage came. Now, arrayed in white satin and pearls, she enters the room, leaning on the arm of Harry.

All eyes were turned towards her, and many compliments were passed. All the color left the cheek of Dora, and her complexion resembled alabaster. Her bright eyes sparkled from 'neath their silken lashes, and a placid smile was on her brow.

Every slave upon the plantation was in the room. Old Aunt Phebe got as near to Dora as she possibly could, and wept while the ceremony was being performed. It was, indeed, an evening of festivity; music and dancing filled the saloons, and every one seemed happy.

Lydia congratulated herself on having the pleasure of calling Dora sister. Now she could be with her always, or, at least, when she could make it convenient.

Harry reflected upon the morning and the accident which led to his meeting with Dora at Niagara, and felt grateful to Heaven for thus ordering it.

That evening, after the company had finished dancing, as they were sitting quite still, being a little fatigued in consequence of dancing so much, they were greeted with music from the banjo. It seems that Ben was determined that the fiddler should not outdo him; and the remainder of the slaves thought they would give the company a specimen of their dancing.

The company were all very much amused at the hilarity of the slaves, and participated in the sight.

Aunt Phebe and Uncle Dick had gone to their cabin, and were expressing their opinions pretty freely upon the marriage.

"I tells yer what, ole ooman, dat young missus ob ourn has got a moughty nice husband. I'se mighty glad on it, for I tinks dat she desarves it. But didn't she look de purtiest dat you eber see anyting."

"I cried, ole man, dat I did, 'caze I was sorry. I knowed dat she had made a good choice, but den I tought ob de time when I used ter nuss her; den jist ter see, now she is married."

"Did you eber see anyting done up at shorter notice? Why, she ain't been from dat ar' school at de Norf more den twelve months, and now she is married."

"I tought she wa'n't gwine ter be long 'bout it, no-how; 'caze yer see all dem dar young gemmen all around here's been courtin' on her all de winter. I tought, when she didn't mind none ob dem, dat she had some notion in her head den."

We will now pass over a little space, about a month after Dora's marriage. Lydia had gone home, as she could not stay any longer at that time. Dora missed her very much, and would have missed her more, had it not been for Harry's company.

It proved a happy marriage, indeed. Harry found that he had made no mistake in his choice, and would not have altered his situation for that of the greatest prince in the world. He felt that he was too happy to wish for the power of the greatest ruler, or the throne of a king.

Mr. M—— had a magnificent mansion erected after the taste of Harry and Dora. A splendid white marble fountain was placed in the garden, and the richest and rarest flowers were planted there. Uncle Dick had obtained a young magnolia-tree from the woods, and placed it in the garden. He was an excellent gardener, and attended strictly to Dora's.

Her home was a perfect little paradise, and the disposition of the happy pair was congenial, and that rendered them thrice happy.

Mr. and Mrs. M—— never had cause to regret the choice Dora had made, and thought that, had she searched the world over, she could not have been better suited.

Charles went to Europe on a tour, and on his way home he paid a visit to Lydia, and shortly after married her. He then brought her to his home in the "sunny South," with which she was perfectly charmed.

Aunt Phebe and Uncle Dick were set free. Mr. and Mrs. M—— agreed that it would be best to give them their freedom, although they did not seem to be very desirous of obtaining it. They had been faithful servants, and, as a reward, a neat little garden and cottage were given them, together with a quantity of poultry, and all the necessary appendages for a market-garden. Aunt Phebe would render her services to Dora, for which she was amply repaid, while Uncle Dick attended to the garden, and kept it in fine order.

The remainder of the slaves remained with Mr. M—— until his death, after which they were disposed of as the will directed.

Ben and Lizzie went to Liberia, and they often received a sum of money from Dora; and ofttimes a letter of encouragement is sent to them.

The summer season was generally spent by Dora at the North, among Harry's relations, who were all very much pleased with the choice he had made, and never regretted that he married the daughter of a slave-holder. Prosperity smiled upon the happy pair, and they were a source of much pleasure to their parents in their old age.

Aunt Phebe and Uncle Dick lived to a good old age, and, when they were about to leave this world, they blessed their owners for having been so kind to them ; and told them that they would meet with their reward both on earth and in heaven, for they had performed their duty faithfully. The aged pair died blessing Harry and Dora, who rejoiced to see them die thus triumphantly, and thanked Heaven for thus having guided them in the proper paths, and for instructing them how it was best for them to perform their duty towards their slaves.

23

CONCLUDING REMARKS.

THE authoress had anticipated writing something on Southern life before she saw or read "Uncle Tom's Cabin." But after the perusal of that overdrawn picture, she really felt it her duty to stand up for her own native place. Mrs. Stowe has certainly represented things in a very different light from what they are. She knows nothing of Southern life, therefore should not attempt to write upon anything of the kind. She would certainly lead persons (who are weak-minded) to believe they are the most inhuman set of people on the earth.

The writer of this has heard many Northern people, who have read "Uncle Tom," say, they have been South, but never saw anything like what Mrs. Stowe represents. We should judge that Mrs. S. was very fond of embellishing; and to that we attribute much that she has said.

The work before you is the first one of the authoress which has appeared in pamphlet form, and the first one of any length. She hopes her readers will bear with the imperfections, and remember that youth is on the side of the author. It is not to be expected that she should write like those who have been making observations for a long time upon the world, for she has left school but two years, and at boarding-school there is but little chance of learning " the ways of the world." She writes this work merely to defend the South. Many would ask if this were a true story. To this the writer would reply, that there are a thousand such instances at the South, where the strong attachment here represented exists between the slave and his owners.

Any one, at the first glance of " Uncle Tom's Cabin," can see that it is written by a strongly prejudiced abolitionist; so, of course, we will have to make allowances for all that is said. Persons are sometimes very apt to dream or imagine things, and they think, as a matter of course, it must be so. This was the case with Mrs. Stowe, when she drew that horrid set of inhuman creatures like Legree. Happily they exist nowhere but in her own imagination.

We are much indebted to Mrs. Mary H. Eastman for correcting one error of Mrs. S., who says that a negro was burned at a certain tree. Mrs. Eastman observes that the tree was struck by lightning, and that is the most probable of the two.

We would merely suggest that Mrs. Stowe has many mistaken ideas of the South and slave-holders. We would most cordially invite her to visit the South, and it is very probable that she would open her eyes, and go to work and alter " Uncle Tom " very quickly.

But the authoress will not dwell upon the subject any longer. She merely wishes to hold up for the South; and she does feel and know that there is not a place on earth where servants are treated more kindly, or have better care taken of them. And if Mrs. Stowe, or any other abolitionist, will come South, we will pretty soon show them what "Southern life" is.   If the Northern people have any sympathy to spare, let them give it to their poor white servants, for our slaves do not stand in any need of it at all.